Instructor's Manual to Accompany

PUBLIC
SPEAKING
in a Free Society

THOMAS L. TEDFORD

University of North Carolina at Greensboro

McGraw-Hill Publishing Company
New York St. Louis San Francisco Auckland Bogotá Caracas
Hamburg Lisbon London Madrid Mexico Milan
Montreal New Delhi Oklahoma City Paris San Juan
São Paulo Singapore Sydney Tokyo Toronto

Instructor's Manual to Accompany
PUBLIC SPEAKING IN A FREE SOCIETY
Copyright ©1991 by McGraw-Hill, Inc. All rights reserved.
Printed in the United States of America. The contents, or
parts thereof, may be reproduced for use with
PUBLIC SPEAKING IN A FREE SOCIETY
by Thomas L. Tedford
provided such reproductions bear copyright notice, but may not
be reproduced in any form for any other purpose without
permission of the publisher.

ISBN 0-07-063389-4

1 2 3 4 5 6 7 8 9 0 W H T W H T 9 5 4 3 2 1

iii

CONTENTS

INTRODUCTION TO THE INSTRUCTOR'S MANUAL

This instructor's manual is designed for all who use <u>Public Speaking in a Free Society</u> as a text for the college-level public speaking course. The manual has four parts, plus two appendices. **Part I** includes suggested goals for the public speaking course, provides two complete course outlines (one for the semester system, and one for the quarter system), and describes a variety of public speaking assignments.

Part II discusses approaches to grading the public speaking course, and gives some practical advice concerning oral and written critiques of student speeches. In addition, five critique forms are provided: one for general use, one for informative speeches, one for visual aids speeches, one for persuasive speeches, and one based on Monroe's motivated sequence. <u>All five critique forms are based on a uniform scoring system</u>, making it convenient for the instructor to switch from form to form without complicating speech grading for the course.

Part III consists of a chapter-by-chapter presentation of goals and projects. The materials for each chapter include a list of goals, a variety of exercises, resources (including videos and filmstrips), and examination questions. The examination questions are of three types: multiple-choice, short answer, and discussion-essay.

Part IV provides two speeches for study and discussion to supplement those that appear in the text. The first is John F. Kennedy's speech on church and state, delivered to the Greater Houston Ministerial Association during the campaign of 1960. The second is a student persuasive speech. Both of the speeches are arranged with a "comments" space on the page to facilitate student analysis and evaluation. They are easily duplicated for distribution to the class.

Two appendices complete the manual. **Appendix I**, "Sources for Resources," provides the addresses of the distributors of videos and filmstrips about public speaking that have been listed in the chapter-by-chapter sections, plus a summary of instructional aids available from the Speech Communication Association. **Appendix II** gives the answers to the examination questions listed in Part III of this manual.

The author is interested in suggestions for improving both the text and the instructor's manual. Instructors who wish to make recommendations concerning future editions of <u>Public Speaking in a Free Society</u> are invited to write as follows:

Thomas L. Tedford
Com. Studies (Ferg. 102)
UNC-Greensboro
Greensboro, N.C. 27412

PART I

SUGGESTED GOALS, COURSE OUTLINES, AND SPEAKING ASSIGNMENTS

The goals, outlines, and speaking assignments detailed below should be adapted to the needs of each instructor and course. By adding, deleting, and shifting, the materials can be quickly and easily adjusted to a variety of instructional situations. For example, the list of goals is derived from the content of <u>Public Speaking in a Free Society</u>; however, the list is not exhaustive, and it is not intended as a substitute for the special requirements of the course as determined by the instructor or the departmental faculty.

Following the statement of goals, two course outlines are provided, one for the semester system (15 weeks), and one for the quarter system (10 weeks). The outlines are developed on the assumption that there are about <u>twenty</u> students in the class, requiring four class hours to complete one speaking assignment (typically, five speakers per class meeting). For larger classes, the instructor will need to adjust the schedule to provide time for the speeches.

Finally, the course outlines are supplemented by the detailed speaking assignments at the end of this part of the manual. Both informative and persuasive assignments are provided. The outlines are further supplemented by Part III of the manual which provides chapter-by-chapter suggestions for the instructor.

Course Goals

This course is planned to help the student achieve the following goals:

1. <u>Historical</u>: to gain an overview of the development of public speaking theory and practice in the West, including the place of public speaking in democratic societies.

2. <u>Theoretical</u>: to know about the body of knowledge called "rhetorical theory" that helps teach a person how to speak clearly and persuasively.

3. <u>Free Speech</u>: to appreciate the importance of freedom of speech in our society, yet to be aware of the legal limitations on free speech as established by the U.S. Supreme Court.

4. Responsible Speech: to consider important issues of communication ethics, and to begin to formulate a set of personal standards for ethics in public speaking.

5. Knowledge and Conviction: to learn the importance of being informed on and having sincere convictions about speech subjects.

6. Audience Analysis: to understand the critical importance of audience analysis in speech planning, and to learn how to do that analysis.

7. Speech Content: to learn how to prepare both informative and persuasive speeches that are clear, logical, well-supported, and well-organized.

8. Delivery: to improve one's ability to deliver a public speech in a confident, effective manner.

9. Reasoning: to improve one's skills of critical thinking.

10. Speech Criticism: to learn the basic principles of speech analysis and evaluation and how to apply this knowledge to speeches heard in class and in society at large.

Course Outlines

Instructor's Outline for a Semester Course
(15 weeks, 45 hours)

This outline provides the student with five speaking experiences: the speech of introduction; two informative speeches (one requiring the use of visual aids); and two persuasive speeches.

Unit I: Introduction to Public Speaking

1. Introduction to the course.

   Distribute the syllabus; explain course policies concerning such things as grading, attendance, and late work. Discuss the first student speech (speech of introduction).

Assign Chapter 1, "The Study of Public Speaking in a Democracy"; also, ask students to begin preparation of the first speech.

2. <u>Our rhetorical heritage: discussion of Chapter 1.</u>

Provide final instructions for the first student speech, and answer questions about it. Then, lead a discussion of Chapter 1, including the historical development of rhetorical theory, the way that democracy creates a need for rhetoric, and the interaction of democracy, rhetoric, and freedom of speech. Relate the chapter to contemporary society, and establish a general tone for the course.

Assign Chapter 2, "Your First Speeches."

3. <u>Speeches of introduction.</u>

Half of the class delivers the speech of introduction.

Assign Chapter 3, "Democratic Values, Free Speech, and Speaker Ethics."

4. <u>Speeches of introduction.</u>

The remaining half of the class speaks.

Assign continued study of Chapter 3.

5. <u>Freedom and responsibility: discussion of Chapter 3.</u>

Lead a discussion of democratic values, freedom of speech, and speaker ethics.

Assign Chapter 4, "The Communication Process and Listening."

6. <u>Communication and listening: discussion of Chapter 4.</u>

Lead a discussion of the communication process, and the basic principles of effective listening. Finish the period with a summary and review of Unit I (Chapters 1, 2, 3, and 4).

7. <u>Examination over Unit I.</u>

Administer examination over first four chapters.

Assign Chapter 5, "Analyzing the Audience and Occasion."

* * * * *

Unit II: Speech Preparation and Speaking to Inform

8. <u>Audience and occasion: discussion of Chapter 5</u>.

    Lead a discussion of audience and occasion analysis. Focus on how to secure and use information about the interests, knowledge, and attitudes of the students in the class who compose the audience for the course.

    Assign Chapter 6, "Determining the Subject and Purpose"; also assign the first informative speech.

9. <u>Subjects and purposes: discussion of Chapter 6</u>.

    Lead a discussion about speech subjects and purposes. Explain the difference between informing and persuading, and relate the discussion to student work on the upcoming speech to inform.

    Assign Chapter 9, "Introducing Outlining: Three Practical Concepts."

10. <u>Introduction to outlining: discussion of Chapter 9</u>.

    Lead a discussion of the speech unit approach to outlining. Explain superior, subordinate, and coordinate relationships, and how to apply the "for" test and the "also" test.

    Assign Chapter 10, "Organizing and Outlining the Body of the Speech."

11. <u>Outlining the body: discussion of Chapter 10</u>.

    Lead a discussion of outlining the body of the speech, including an explanation of speech patterns. Apply chapter material to the upcoming informative speech by carefully going over the model outline at the end of the chapter (informative speech on "Fair Use"). Use the model outline to establish a standard style for all outlines in the course.

    Assign Chapter 11, "Introductions, Conclusions, and Transitions."

12. <u>Outlining introductions and conclusions: discussion of Chapter 11</u>.

    Lead a discussion of planning introductions and conclusions, with special attention to introducing and concluding the speech to inform. Discuss transitions. Use the model outline at the end of Chapter 10 to illustrate style for outlining the introduction and the conclusion.

    Assign Chapter 14, "Speaking to Inform."

13. <u>Informative speaking: discussion of Chapter 14</u>.

    Lead a discussion of informative speaking, beginning with the materials on finding good subjects. Go over the principles of motivation, clarification, and retention.

    Assign Chapter 12, "Language in Public Speaking."

14. <u>Language in public speaking: discussion of Chapter 12</u>.

    Lead a discussion of language, covering the semantic and stylistic functions of language in public speaking.

    Assign Chapter 13, "Delivering the Speech," and Appendix II, "Extemporaneous Speaking: Model Outlines, Notecards, and Speeches."

15. <u>Speech delivery: discussion of Chapter 13</u>.

    Lead a discussion of speech delivery, with an emphasis on extemporaneous speaking using note cards. Go over the model informative outline, note cards, and speech in Appendix II.

16. <u>Speech to inform</u>.

    First round of informative speeches.

    Assign the next speech (informative, requiring the use of visual aids). Ask students to begin work on the second speech as soon as they can.

17. <u>Speech to inform</u>.

    Second round of informative speeches.

18. <u>Speech to inform</u>.

   Third round of informative speeches.

   Assign Chapter 7, "Supporting Materials for Public Speeches."

19. <u>Speech to inform</u>.

   Final round of informative speeches.

   Assign continued study of Chapter 7.

20. <u>Supporting materials and visual aids: discussion of Chapter 7</u>.

   Lead a discussion of supporting materials and visual aids.

   Assignment: students should continue to work on the visual aids speech.

21. <u>Final discussion of visual aids speech</u>.

   Lead the final discussion on the visual aids speech. Review the requirements for the speech, and answer student questions.

22. <u>Visual aids speech to inform</u>.

   First round of visual aids speeches.

   Announce the mid-term examination.

23. <u>Visual aids speech to inform</u>.

   Second round of visual aids speeches.

24. <u>Visual aids speech to inform</u>.

   Third round of visual aids speeches.

25. <u>Visual aids speech to inform</u>.

   Final round of visual aids speeches.

26. <u>Summary and review of the unit</u>.

27. <u>Mid-term examination</u>.

   Assign Chapter 15, "The Means of Persuasion."

   *   *   *   *   *

**Unit III: Speech Preparation and
Speaking to Persuade**

28. <u>Logical proof in persuasion: discussion of Chapter 15</u>.

Introduce persuasive speaking by announcing the two
persuasive speeches that will complete the course.
Lead a discussion of the first part of Chapter 15
concerning logical reasoning and persuasion.

Assign continued study of Chapter 15.

29. <u>Ethical and emotional proofs in persuasion: continued
discussion of Chapter 15</u>.

Lead a discussion of the second and third parts of
Chapter 15 concerning speaker credibility and
psychological appeals (emotions, needs, and values) in
persuasion. Apply the theory of Chapter 15 to the
upcoming speeches.

Assign Chapter 16, "Speaking to Persuade."

30. <u>Types of persuasive speeches: discussion of Chapter
16</u>.

Lead a discussion of types of persuasive speeches (to
convince, to actuate, and to reinforce). Apply to the
two persuasive speeches that students are to deliver.

Assign continued study of Chapter 16.

31. <u>Approaches to persuasion: continued discussion of
Chapter 16</u>.

Lead a discussion of the various research-based
approaches to persuasive speaking that are explained in
Chapter 16. Apply the material to the upcoming
speeches.

**Assign Appendix I, "Speech Criticism: Analyzing and
Evaluating Public Speeches."**

32. <u>Speech criticism: first discussion of Appendix I</u>.

Lead a discussion of the fundamentals of speech
criticism, based upon Appendix I. Explain the short
critique form and its use in class (the long form is
included in the text; the short form can be found at
the end of the chapter-by-chapter discussion, Part III
of this manual).

Assign the final persuasive speech.

33. Speech to persuade.

First round of persuasive speeches (with student critiques using the short form).

34. Speech to persuade.

Second round of persuasive speeches (with student critiques).

35. Speech to persuade.

Third round of persuasive speeches (with student critiques).

Assign a review of Chapter 15, "The Means of Persuasion."

36. Speech to persuade.

Final round of persuasive speeches (with student critiques).

Assign a review of Chapter 16, "Speaking to Persuade."

37. Instructions and discussion of the final persuasive speech.

Explain and discuss the final speech, answering student questions concerning the project.

Assign a review of Appendix I on speech criticism.

38. Speech criticism: second discussion of Appendix I.

Discuss speech criticism for the second time, using the experiences of the class in analyzing and evaluating the persuasive speeches just completed. Go over the long critique form, and prepare students for using the long form for critiquing the final speeches.

39. Final speech to persuade.

First round of final speeches (with student critiques using the long form).

40. Final speech to persuade.

Second round of final speeches (with student critiques).

41. Final speech to persuade.

Third round of final speeches (with student critiques).

42. <u>Final speech to persuade</u>.

Fourth round of final speeches (with student critiques).

43. <u>Final speech to persuade</u>.

Fifth round of final speeches (with student critiques).

44. <u>Open date</u>.

Use this date for the delivery of late speeches and any other "catch up" activities or discussions that are needed.

45. <u>Summary of course and review for the final exam</u>.

FINAL EXAMINATION

Instructor's Outline for a Quarter Course
(10 weeks, 30 hours)

This outline provides the student with four speaking experiences: a speech of introduction; an informative speech using visual aids; and two persuasive speeches.

Unit I: Introduction to Public Speaking

1. <u>Introduction to the course</u>.

Distribute the syllabus; explain course policies on such matters as grading, attendance, and late work. Alert students to first classroom speech (the speech of introduction), and discuss it briefly.

Assign Chapter 1, "The Study of Public Speaking in a Democracy." Also, assign dates for the speech of introduction.

2. <u>Our rhetorical heritage: discussion of Chapter 1</u>.

    Provide final instructions for the first student
    speech, and answer questions about it. Then, lead a
    discussion of Chapter 1, including the historical
    development of rhetorical theory, the way that
    democracy creates a need for rhetoric, and the
    interaction of democracy, rhetoric, and freedom of
    speech. Relate the chapter to contemporary society,
    and establish a general tone for the course.

    Assign Chapter 2, "Your First Speeches."

3. <u>Speeches of introduction</u>.

    Half of the class delivers the speech of introduction.

    Assign Chapter 3, "Democratic Values, Free Speech, and
    Speaker Ethics."

4. <u>Speeches of introduction</u>.

    The remaining half of the class speaks.

    Assign continued study of Chapter 3.

5. <u>Freedom and responsibility: discussion of Chapter 3</u>.

    Lead a discussion of democratic values, freedom of
    speech, and speaker ethics.

    Assign Chapter 4, "The Communication Process and
    Listening."

6. <u>Communication and listening: discussion of Chapter 4</u>.

    Lead a discussion of the communication process, and the
    basic principles of effective listening.

    Assign Chapter 5, "Analyzing the Audience and
    Occasion."

                    *   *   *   *   *

**Unit II: Speech Preparation and
Speaking to Inform**

7.   <u>Audience and occasion: discussion of Chapter 5</u>.

     Lead a discussion of audience and occasion analysis.
     Focus on how to secure and use information about the
     interests, knowledge, and attitudes of the students in
     the class who compose the audience for the course.

     Assign Chapter 6, "Determining the Subject and
     Purpose"; also assign the visual aids speech.

8.   <u>Subjects and purposes: discussion of Chapter 6</u>.

     Lead a discussion about speech subjects and purposes.
     Explain the difference between informing and
     persuading, and relate the content of Chapter 6 to the
     three student speeches that follow (one to inform, and
     two to persuade).

     Assign Chapter 9, "Introducing Outlining: Three
     Practical Concepts," and Chapter 10, "Organizing and
     Outlining the Body of the Speech."

9.   <u>Outlining the speech: discussion of Chapters 9 and 10</u>.

     Lead the first discussion of outlining, drawing on the
     content of Chapter 9 to establish a foundation for
     logical organization. The discussion continues into
     next class period.

     Assign Chapter 11, "Introductions, Conclusions, and
     Transitions."

10. <u>Outlining the speech continued: discussion of Chapters
     9, 10, and 11</u>.

     Continue the discussion of logical outlining. Use the
     model outline at the end of Chapter 10 to establish a
     standard style for all outlines in the course.

     Assign Chapter 7, "Supporting Materials for Public
     Speeches," and Chapter 14, "Speaking to Inform."

11. <u>Informative speaking and visual aids: discussion of Chapters 7 and 14</u>.

Lead a discussion of supporting materials, visual aids, and the speech to inform.

Assign Chapter 12, "Language in Public Speaking," and Chapter 13, "Delivering the Speech." Also, ask students to review Appendix II, "Extemporaneous Speaking: Model Outlines, Note Cards, and Speeches."

12. <u>Language and delivery: discussion of Chapters 12 and 13</u>.

Lead a discussion of language and delivery, with an emphasis on extemporaneous speaking using note cards. Use the information in Appendix II to illustrate the points being made.

13. <u>Visual aids speech to inform</u>.

First round of visual aids speeches.

Announce the mid-term examination.

14. <u>Visual aids speech to inform</u>.

Second round of visual aids speeches.

15. <u>Visual aids speech to inform</u>.

Third round of visual aids speeches.

16. <u>Visual aids speech to inform</u>.

Final round of visual aids speeches.

17. <u>Mid-term examination</u>.

Assign Appendix I, "Speech Criticism: Analyzing and Evaluating Public Speeches."

* * * * *

**Unit III: Speech Preparation and
Speaking to Persuade**

18. <u>Instructions for the two persuasive speeches and a
    discussion of speech criticism</u>.

    Preview the unit. Announce the two persuasive
    speeches, and go over the requirements for both.
    Assign speaking dates for the first persuasive speech.
    Discuss Appendix I on speech criticism. If student
    critiques of persuasive speeches are planned, explain
    the forms to be used (long form, as in the text; or
    short form, found at the end of Part III of this
    manual).

    Assign Chapter 15, "The Means of Persuasion."

19. <u>Logical proof in persuasion: discussion of Chapter 15</u>.

    Go over first persuasive speech again, answering
    student questions. Then lead a discussion of the first
    part of Chapter 15 concerning logical reasoning and
    persuasion.

    Assign continued study of Chapter 15.

20. <u>Ethical and emotional proofs: continued discussion of
    Chapter 15</u>.

    Lead a discussion of the second and third parts of
    Chapter 15 concerning speaker credibility and
    psychological appeals (emotions, needs, and values) in
    persuasive speaking. Apply the theory of Chapter 15 to
    the upcoming speeches.

    Assign Chapter 16, "Speaking to Persuade."

21. <u>Types of persuasive speeches: discussion of Chapter
    16</u>.

    Lead a discussion of types of persuasive speeches, and
    approaches to persuasion, based on chapter content.
    Apply the theory of Chapter 16 to the upcoming
    speeches.

    Assign speaking dates for the final persuasive speech.

22. <u>Speech to persuade</u>.

    First round of persuasive speeches.

    Assign a review of Chapter 15 during the first two
    rounds of speaking.

23. <u>Speech to persuade</u>.

   Second round of persuasive speeches.

24. <u>Speech to persuade</u>.

   Third round of persuasive speeches.

   Assign a review of Chapter 16 during the final two
   rounds of speaking.

25. <u>Speech to persuade</u>.

   Final round of persuasive speeches.

26. <u>Discussion of final speech and review for the final
   examination</u>.

   Go over the requirements of the final persuasive
   speech. Explain the student critiques, based upon the
   content of Appendix I. Pass out copies of the critique
   form that will be used. Announce the final
   examination, and review materials that should be
   studied.

27. <u>Final speech to persuade</u>.

   First round of final speeches (with student critiques).

28. <u>Final speech to persuade</u>.

   Second round of final speeches (with student
   critiques).

29. <u>Final speech to persuade</u>.

   Third round of final speeches (with student critiques).

30. <u>Final speech to persuade</u>.

   Fourth round of final speeches (with student
   critiques).

FINAL EXAMINATION

Speaking Assignments

The suggested speaking assignments explained below cover the
five speeches for the course outline based on the semester
system. Those who teach on the quarter system will need to
cut one of the assignments (such as the first informative
speech).

Speech of Introduction

Option A

Students should prepare a 2 to 3 minute speech of
self-introduction, providing the class with "get acquainted"
information about themselves, such as name, home community,
hobbies and interests, academic major and career plans, and
why they chose this particular college or university. The
speech should be delivered extemporaneously. No outline is
required, although a single topical note card is permitted.
To help the speakers relax with the first assignment, the
speech should be ungraded. For suggestions, the students
can review the discussion about "Introducing Yourself to
Others" in Chapter 2.

Option B

Assign each student a classmate to introduce. Students
should interview the person to whom they are assigned,
securing information about that person's home community,
hobbies and interests, academic major and career plans, and
so forth. From the information gained, prepare a 2 to 3
minute speech introducing that student to the class. The
speech should be delivered extemporaneously. No outline is
required, although a single note card is permitted. The
speech should be ungraded. For suggestions, the students
can review the material on "Introducing Other Persons" in
Chapter 2.

Option C

This assignment can be completed in one class period rather
than two as required by the options above (thereby saving a
day for optional activity). To do this, have 1 to 2 minute
impromptu introductions. At the beginning of the period,
write these topics on the board:

      Name and Home Town
      Hobbies and Interests
      College Major and Career Plans
      Your Primary Goal/s in This Course

Explain that the talk is not being graded, then have each
student do a brief self-introduction on the topics listed.

First Speech to Inform

Option A

Assign a 5 to 6 minute informative speech on a subject of the student's choice. The speech can be about people, events, definitions and concepts, processes or procedures, objects, or places. The subject should not be trivial, and it should be of interest to those in the class. For ideas on informative subjects, the student should see Chapters 6 and 14. A sentence outline is to be submitted prior to the delivery of the speech. The speech should be delivered extemporaneously; note cards are permitted. The speech is graded.

Option B

In contrast to Option A, which permits a wide range of subject choice, assign a 5 to 6 minute informative speech of a specific type, such as one explaining a process or procedure, or one explaining a definition or concept. A sentence outline should be submitted to the instructor before the speech is delivered. Delivery should be extemporaneous with note cards permitted. The speech is graded.

Visual Aids Speech to Inform

Option A

Assign a 5 to 6 minute informative speech on a subject of the student's choice. The student must employ visual aids that he or she has prepared for this specific speech. Charts, graphs, diagrams, maps, or models built by the student are recommended. The visual aid should help explain significant points of the body of the speech, and should not be "tacked on" as a mere technicality of meeting the requirements of the assignment. The visuals should meet the standards described in Chapter 7 of the text. A sentence outline is required. The speech should be delivered extemporaneously. Note cards are permitted.

Option B

As an option, permit more flexibility in the choice of visual aids by announcing that the visuals can be either prepared by the student, or prepared by others (such as instructional charts used in a course, or professionally made models that the student can borrow). Otherwise, the assignment would be the same as in Option A.

First Speech to Persuade

Option A

Assign a 5 to 6 minute persuasive speech to convince or to actuate on a subject that concerns the students in the class. Campus issues, problems of student life, or issues that concern the local community are particularly appropriate for this assignment. A sentence outline is required. Claims made in the speech should be supported with evidence, and the sources of the evidence should be qualified. Delivery should be extemporaneous, with note cards permitted. Visual aids may be used if needed, but their use is optional.

Option B

Assign a 5 to 6 minute persuasive speech of good will. (This option is particularly appropriate for students planning careers in public relations, because creating good will is an inherent part of the work of the public relations professional.) In preparation, students should study the discussion of the good will speech in Chapter 17. The speech can aim toward creating good will toward a cause, organization, institution, business, or profession. A sentence outline is required. Delivery should be extemporaneous, with note cards permitted.

Option C

Assign a 5 to 6 minute eulogy, a special type of speech to inspire. The student should select a deceased person whom they admire, study that person's life, and prepare a speech praising that person's character and achievements.   In preparation, students should study the discussion of the eulogy in Chapter 17. A sentence outline is required. Delivery should be extemporaneous, with note cards permitted.

Final Speech
Second Speech to Persuade

Option A

Assign a 6 to 8 minute persuasive speech of policy. The speech, which may be either to convince or to actuate, should address a significant contemporary problem, analyze it, and propose a solution (that is, a policy) that will solve or help solve the problem. This speech is to be based on research and documented with a minimum of eight good sources. (Suggest that a review of Chapter 8, "Research: Finding Speech Materials," is in order for this assignment.)

A sentence outline is required, and <u>a bibliography of sources is to be attached to the outline</u>. Claims made in the speech, and proposals to solve the problem, are to be supported with evidence. The evidence should be carefully qualified by the speaker as the speech is being presented. Delivery should be extemporaneous, with note cards permitted. Visual aids may be used if needed; however, the use of visuals is optional.

<u>Option B</u>

Assign a 6 to 8 minute persuasive speech of policy to be <u>delivered from a manuscript</u>. This project is the same as Option A except that <u>both a sentence outline and a complete manuscript are required</u>. The manuscript should be carefully documented with footnotes (or endnotes), and a bibliography of at least eight good sources should be attached to it. For delivery, the speech is to be read from the manuscript. In preparation for this assignment, the student should study the discussion of manuscript delivery in Chapter 13. Remind the students that they should rehearse with the manuscript several times before the speech is presented to the class.

PART II

GRADING AND SPEECH CRITICISM

Grading

Grading the course in public speaking should be based
on student mastery of both the theory and practice of public
speaking. Some instructors put an equal emphasis on theory
and practice in determining the final grade, designating
half of the grade for written assignments and examinations,
and half for the delivered speeches. Others prefer to weigh
the speeches more heavily than other assignments, providing
for a greater percentage of the grade to be based on
practice. Here are examples that illustrate both
approaches.

Course A: a 50/50 proportion

1.   Examinations and written assignments, 50 percent
     of course grade.
     a.   Unit I exam, 10%.
     b.   Unit II exam, 10%.
     c.   Other written assignments, 10%.
     d.   Final examination, 20%.
2.   Speeches, 50 percent of course grade.
     There will be four graded speeches; the instructor
     will grade each speech, consider overall
     improvement, and assign a value to this half of
     the course.

Course B: a 40/60 proportion

1.   Examinations and written assignments, 40 percent
     of course grade.
     a.   Mid-term exam, 10%.
     b.   Other written assignments, 10%.
     c.   Final examination, 20%.
2.   Speeches, 60 percent of course grade.
     There will be four graded speeches; the instructor
     will grade each speech, consider overall
     improvement, and assign a value to this 60 percent
     of the course.

The section on delivered speeches can be described in
general terms, as is done above, or can be made specific.
For example, part two of Course A could be detailed this
way: 10 percent for each of the four speeches, plus 10
percent for overall improvement, resulting in a total of 50
percent. The method adopted should be fully explained to
the class at the beginning of the course. Many instructors
include this information in the syllabus.

Specific suggestions for written assignments and examinations are detailed in Part III of this manual where a variety of exercises and test questions are provided, chapter by chapter. The grading of speeches is discussed below.

Speech Criticism

Criticizing student speeches and assigning speech grades are challenges to the instructor of the public speaking course. In Appendix I of Public Speaking in a Free Society, speech criticism is defined as informed, fair-minded analysis and evaluation of a speech. The critic does analysis by explaining what is going on in the speech, and why it works or does not work; and the critic does evaluation by making informed judgments of the effectiveness, artistic quality, and social worth of a speech. The instructor of a public speaking course should employ both analysis and evaluation when commenting on student speeches.

To help the student improve his or her speech presentation, the instructor should try to provide both written and oral comments for each speech delivered (or, at least for the major speeches). To accomplish this, the number of speeches planned for a given day must be limited in order to provide time for oral criticism. Some instructors like to comment immediately after a speech is delivered, whereas others prefer to wait until after all of the day's speeches have been delivered. A variation is to have the complete round of speeches delivered before giving criticism (for example, have all speeches delivered in two periods, spending the third period giving oral critiques and returning the written criticism forms with speech grades assigned). The type of grade assigned merits special attention.

Grading the Speech:
Letter Grade vs. a Score

Many students are tense, nervous, and ego-involved about speaking in public. Although they need constructive criticism, they are often sensitive to it. Giving a student a traditional letter grade, such as a B, C, or D, on a speech evokes a predictable response, often negative, causing the student to focus on the grade instead of the areas of speaking that need improvement. In such instances the student is likely to say, "I made a D," when, instead, he or she should be saying "I need to choose better speech subjects," or "I need to improve my outlines." One way to avoid this problem is to use a nontraditional grading system for the speeches, such as a score rather than a letter grade.

The use of a score for grading is facilitated by a system based on a five-point scale that equates roughly to the traditional lettering system. For example, 1 compares to F, 2 to D, 3 to C, 4 to B, and 5 to A. When this scale is used on a ten-item critique form (see the critique forms at the end of this section of the manual), a score of 10 on a speech equates roughly to F, 20 to D, 30 to C, 40 to B, and 50 to A. However, the instructor need not convert the scores to letter grades--at least not early in the course. A descriptive term, such as those below, can be used instead.

Single items (such as "Choice of Subject") marked with a 1 are **poor**; speeches earning 10 points are **poor**.

Single items marked with a 2 are **fair**; speeches earning 20 points are **fair**.

Single items marked with a 3 are **average**; speeches earning 30 points are **average**.

Single items marked with a 4 are **good**; speeches earning 40 points are **good**.

Single items marked with a 5 are **excellent**; speeches earning 50 points are **excellent**.

All five critique forms at the end of this part of the manual use these descriptive terms and numbers. This uniformity means that the instructor can switch from one form to another during the course while retaining the basic scale described above. Thus, an informative speech graded with Form B, and receiving a score of 30, is "average," as is a persuasive speech graded with Form D and receiving a score of 30.

Instructors who grade speeches with scores rather than letters need not total the scores and divide by the number of speeches to get a mean score at the end of the course (although this is one option). Instead, the improvement in the scores can be tracked and the final grade for classroom speeches assigned based on overall improvement rather than an average. For example, a student whose four speeches are scored at 25, 30, 38, and 45 has shown definite improvement, going from "below average" to "good-plus." For this improvement, the instructor might assign a letter grade of B or B+. On the other hand, a student whose four speeches are scored at 30, 32, 25, and 28 has failed to show overall improvement. For this set of scores, the instructor might assign a letter grade of D+ to C-.

Instructors who prefer to assign a traditional letter grade to each speech will find that the critique forms in this manual adapt easily to such a system.

Critiquing Student Speeches

The criticism of classroom speeches is an important part of teaching the public speaking course. To begin with, the instructor should pay special attention to building his or her own ethos with the students--that is, to establish himself or herself as a person of friendship and good will who has a knowledge of rhetorical theory. After establishing one's credibility, and developing a pleasant, relaxed learning atmosphere, the instructor still has the task of providing specific written and oral criticisms. Here are some thoughts on the matter, dealing first with the principles of criticism, then looking at some practical techniques for putting those principles to work in the classroom.

Principles of Effective Criticism

The instructor's comments on classroom speeches should conform to three important principles of effective criticism, namely, the criticism should be objective, constructive, and definite. Let us look further at each of these principles.

First, the instructor's criticism should be objective, using professional standards derived from sound rhetorical theory as the basis of the criticism. Also, objectivity means that the comments are not personal. In short, the instructor should try to help each student in the class become a more effective public speaker, no matter what subjective or "personal" feelings might exist.

Second, the instructor's criticism should be constructive. Constructive criticism emphasizes the positive, calls attention to strong points as well as weak ones, and explains in clear terms what can be done to improve. Such criticism helps to build, not to tear down. Among other things, the instructor works with students in such a way that each student is receptive to criticism--and wants more of it.

Finally, the instructor's criticism should be definite, not abstract and vague. For example, the instructor who comments that "the speech was pretty good, but could be better," is not being definite. Good in what way? And, in specific terms, what should be done to make the next speech "better"? The instructor could be more specific, and thus more helpful to the student, by commenting: "the delivery was direct and lively, but the organization of the body needs to be more logical."

Techniques of Effective Criticism

There are a number of specific techniques that the instructor can employ to help make speech criticism effective. Here are six (including some mentioned or alluded to above) worth considering.

1. <u>Demonstrate a sincere desire to help</u>. The instructor should develop a teaching approach that communicates a helpful attitude to the class. This can begin early in the course with an explanation of speech criticism (from the text, Appendix I on speech criticism should be useful here). This explanation can include a discussion of the critique sheets to be used in the course, and the nature and goals of both written and oral criticism. Also, an open discussion on the subject by the entire class often helps students develop a positive attitude toward criticism.

2. <u>Start with a positive note</u>. Always jot down a compliment or two on the written critique form. Recognize improvement with an encouraging "pat on the back." Use the same technique when giving oral criticism, starting with comments about the strong points of the speech, then moving diplomatically to a discussion of the weak points.

3. <u>Make clear that the speaker is not alone</u>. Let the student who has a problem know that many others, including great speakers, struggled with the same problem. For example, to the student who talks too fast, the instructor might say, "In his early political career, John F. Kennedy often talked so rapidly that his audience did not understand him. With the help of expert speech critics, and with practice, he overcame this problem to become an outstanding public speaker. You, too, can learn to slow down."

4. <u>Attribute the suggestion to an authority</u>. The instructor can attribute a critical comment or a suggestion for improvement to some other person, thereby directing some of student concern away from the instructor. For instance, the teacher might say, "The great speaker William Jennings Bryan once remarked . . . ," or "My major professor in graduate school often told us in the advanced public speaking class that . . . ." This technique helps keep the instructor

from "bearing all the blame" for the criticisms made in the course.

5.   Phrase the problem as a question.   By asking questions, the instructor can get students involved in discussing their own problems.   Often, the student will identify and analyze a problem better than the instructor.   For instance, the instructor might ask the student struggling with stage fright, "Mary, what are your feelings about speaking before an audience?   Does the thought of making a speech make you nervous?"

6.   Involve others.   The instructor should promote a general spirit of helpfulness in the classroom--one that says, in effect, "we are all in this together, and we are here to help each other."   By occasionally calling on students to make constructive comments, the instructor can involve everyone in the class in the activity of speech criticism.   At times, student critics will "get through" to other students even better than the instructor, thereby enriching the classroom learning experience.

The Critique Forms

As noted earlier, the five critique forms that follow are based on parallel scales.   There are five levels of evaluation (from **poor** to **excellent**) and ten items to be evaluated (from **choice of subject** to **overall effectiveness**) on each form.   This uniformity facilitates grading for the instructor who prefers to use several forms, each tailored to the type of speech being evaluated.   The term "comments" is used in each heading because it is a neutral term that has few, if any, negative connotations (contrasted, for example, with terms such as "criticism" and "critique" that do stir negative feelings in some students).

Form A, "Public Speaking Comments," is designed for general use throughout the course.   It can be employed for all speaking assignments, both informative and persuasive. However, for those who prefer "custom" critique forms, four others are provided: Form B is designed for informative speeches in general; Form C is for informative speeches requiring the use of visual aids; Form D is for persuasive speeches in general; and Form E is for persuasive speeches that are based on Monroe's motivated sequence.

PUBLIC SPEAKING COMMENTS
Analysis and Evaluation

Speaker:_____ Date:_____

1. **CHOICE OF SUBJECT** 1 2 3 4 5
   Appropriate to speaker
   Appropriate to audience
   Appropriate to occasion
2. **OUTLINE FORM** 1 2 3 4 5
   Correct form
   Complete sentences
   Grammar & spelling
3. **DEVELOPMENT OF INTRODUCTION** 1 2 3 4 5
   Gain attention
   Orient to topic
   Clear central idea
4. **DEVELOPMENT OF BODY** 1 2 3 4 5
   Main points
   Support
   Logic & clarity
   Interest materials
5. **DEVELOPMENT OF CONCLUSION** 1 2 3 4 5
   Summary
   Clarity & persuasiveness
   Originality
6. **BODILY COMMUNICATION** 1 2 3 4 5
   Posture
   Visual directness
   Movement & gesture
7. **LANGUAGE AND VOCABULARY** 1 2 3 4 5
   Appropriate
   Clear
   Vivid
8. **VOICE AND ARTICULATION** 1 2 3 4 5
   Rate & pitch
   Quality & loudness
   Distinct articulation
9. **PRONUNCIATION** 1 2 3 4 5

10. **OVERALL EFFECTIVENESS** 1 2 3 4 5
    Speaker credibility
    Clarity & interest
    Persuasiveness
    Social consequences

General comments:

TOTAL SCORE:_____

10 = poor; 20 = fair; 30 = average; 40 = good; 50 = excellent
(Form A)

INFORMATIVE SPEAKING COMMENTS
Analysis and Evaluation

Speaker:_____Date:_____

1. **CHOICE OF SUBJECT** 1 2 3 4 5
   Appropriate to speaker
   Appropriate to audience
   Appropriate to occasion
2. **OUTLINE FORM** 1 2 3 4 5
   Correct form
   Complete sentences
   Grammar & spelling
3. **DEVELOPMENT OF INTRODUCTION** 1 2 3 4 5
   Gain attention
   Orient to topic
   Motivate learning
   Clear central idea & preview
4. **DEVELOPMENT OF BODY** 1 2 3 4 5
   Main points
   Supporting material
   Clarity
   Interest
5. **DEVELOPMENT OF CONCLUSION** 1 2 3 4 5
   Summary
   Clarity
   Originality
6. **BODILY COMMUNICATION** 1 2 3 4 5
   Posture
   Visual directness
   Movement & gesture
7. **LANGUAGE AND VOCABULARY** 1 2 3 4 5
   Appropriate
   Clear
   Vivid
8. **VOICE AND ARTICULATION** 1 2 3 4 5
   Rate & pitch
   Quality & loudness
   Distinct articulation
9. **PRONUNCIATION** 1 2 3 4 5

10. **OVERALL EFFECTIVENESS** 1 2 3 4 5
    Speaker credibility
    Holding interest
    Overall motivation
    Overall clarity
    Summaries (retention)

General comments:

TOTAL SCORE:_____

10 = poor; 20 = fair; 30 = average; 40 = good; 50 = excellent
(Form B)

VISUAL AIDS SPEAKING COMMENTS
Analysis and Evaluation

Speaker:_____ Date:_____

1. **CHOICE OF SUBJECT** 1 2 3 4 5
    Appropriate to speaker
    Appropriate to audience
    Appropriate to occasion
2. **OUTLINE FORM** 1 2 3 4 5
    Correct form
    Complete sentences
    Grammar & spelling
3. **DEVELOPMENT OF INTRODUCTION** 1 2 3 4 5
    Gain attention
    Orient to topic
    Motivate learning
    Clear central idea & preview
4. **DEVELOPMENT OF BODY** 1 2 3 4 5
    Main points
    Supporting material
    Clarity
    Interest
5. **DEVELOPMENT OF CONCLUSION** 1 2 3 4 5
    Summary
    Clarity
    Originality
6. **VISUAL AIDS** 1 2 3 4 5
    Explains important content
    Clarity
    Details easy to see
    Used well by speaker
7. **BODILY COMMUNICATION** 1 2 3 4 5
    Posture
    Visual directness
    Movement & gesture
8. **LANGUAGE AND VOCABULARY** 1 2 3 4 5
    Appropriate
    Clear
    Vivid
9. **VOICE AND DICTION** 1 2 3 4 5
    Rate & pitch
    Quality & loudness
    Distinct articulation
    Standard pronunciation
10. **OVERALL EFFECTIVENESS** 1 2 3 4 5
    Speaker credibility
    Holding interest
    Overall motivation
    Overall clarity
    Summaries (retention)

General comments:

TOTAL SCORE:_____

10 = poor; 20 = fair; 30 = average; 40 = good; 50 = excellent
(Form C)

PERSUASIVE SPEAKING COMMENTS
Analysis and Evaluation

Speaker:_____Date:_____

1. **CHOICE OF SUBJECT** 1 2 3 4 5
   Appropriate to speaker
   Appropriate to audience
   Appropriate to occasion

2. **OUTLINE FORM** 1 2 3 4 5
   Correct form
   Complete sentences
   Grammar & spelling

3. **INTRODUCTION** 1 2 3 4 5
   Gain attention
   Orient to topic
   Build credibility
   Clear central idea

4. **BODY: LOGICAL SUPPORT** 1 2 3 4 5
   Logical main points
   Sound reasoning
   Sound evidence
   Clarity

5. **BODY: OTHER SUPPORTS** 1 2 3 4 5
   Sustain speaker expertise
   Sustain good will
   Appeals to emotions, needs, values
   Interest materials

6. **CONCLUSION** 1 2 3 4 5
   Summary & overall clarity
   Persuasiveness
   Originality

7. **BODILY COMMUNICATION** 1 2 3 4 5
   Posture
   Visual directness
   Movement & gesture

8. **LANGUAGE AND VOCABULARY** 1 2 3 4 5
   Appropriate
   Clear
   Vivid

9. **VOICE AND DICTION** 1 2 3 4 5
   Rate & pitch
   Quality & loudness
   Distinct articulation
   Standard pronunciation

10. **OVERALL EFFECTIVENESS** 1 2 3 4 5
    Speaker credibility
    Persuasiveness
    Clarity & interest
    Social consequences

General comments:

                              TOTAL SCORE:_____

10 = poor; 20 = fair; 30 = average; 40 = good; 50 = excellent
(Form D)

MOTIVATED SEQUENCE PERSUASIVE SPEAKING COMMENTS
Analysis and Evaluation

Speaker: _____ Date: _____

1. **CHOICE OF SUBJECT** 1 2 3 4 5
    Appropriate to speaker
    Appropriate to audience
    Appropriate to occasion
2. **OUTLINE FORM** 1 2 3 4 5
    Correct form
    Complete sentences
    Grammar & spelling
3. **INTRODUCTION: ATTENTION** 1 2 3 4 5
    Gain attention
    Orient to topic
    Build credibility
    Clear central idea
4. **BODY: NEED** 1 2 3 4 5
    Need made clear
    Need made convincing
    Need made relevant to audience
5. **BODY: SATISFACTION** 1 2 3 4 5
    Plan made clear
    Show that plan solves need
    Show that plan is practical
6. **BODY: VISUALIZATION** 1 2 3 4 5
    Benefits made clear
    Benefits follow from plan
    Benefits made vivid
7. **CONCLUSION: ACTION** 1 2 3 4 5
    Persuasive summary
    Appeal for specific action
    Originality of appeal
8. **BODILY COMMUNICATION** 1 2 3 4 5
    Posture
    Visual directness
    Movement & gesture
9. **LANGUAGE, VOICE, AND DICTION** 1 2 3 4 5
    Clear, vivid language
    Vocal variety & loudness
    Distinct articulation
    Standard pronunciation
10. **OVERALL EFFECTIVENESS** 1 2 3 4 5
    Speaker credibility
    Persuasiveness
    Clarity & interest
    Social consequences

General comments:

TOTAL SCORE: _____

10 = poor; 20 = fair; 30 = average; 40 = good; 50 = excellent
(Form E)

PART III

GOALS AND PROJECTS CHAPTER BY CHAPTER

Part III of this manual is a chapter-by-chapter presentation of ideas and suggestions for the public speaking instructor who uses Public Speaking in a Free Society as a basic text. Each chapter presentation covers five topics: chapter goals, ideas for using exercises from the text, additional exercises and activities, resource materials, and test questions. Let us look briefly at each of these five areas.

First, the presentation begins with a set of chapter goals that are stated in terms of student achievement. The instructor who wishes to communicate these goals to the class can do so in a variety of ways, such as by lecture, by writing them on the board, or by giving photocopies to each student. After they have been communicated, they can be used as the basis for a classroom discussion if the instructor so desires.

Second, the exercises that are provided at the end of each chapter in the text are restated here. This is done for the instructor's convenience, so that all suggested exercises (including new ones) are together in the manual for easy reference. Although the exercises in the text are designed for independent use by the students, they are also useful for assignment by the instructor. As a rule, after the textbook exercise is restated, a brief comment is added in the manual suggesting how the instructor can use the exercise as an assigned project.

Third, additional exercises and activities are provided for each chapter. Also, ideas for the instructor, such as lecture topics or questions for classroom discussion, are included in this section.

Fourth, selected resource materials are listed. The materials include a mixture of readings from the lists at the end of each chapter in the text, and new readings not listed in the text. Selected educational **films and videos** are also listed, appearing in **boldface** type at the end of each reading list.

Fifth, three types of test questions are provided: multiple-choice, short answer, and discussion and essay. Occasionally there is an overlap between the questions in the three categories; therefore, instructors should check chosen questions carefully to avoid unwanted content duplication. The instructor who prefers to develop his or her own examinations can use the questions given here as a source of ideas.

Chapter 1

The Study of Public Speaking in a Democracy

Chapter Goals

The content of Chapter 1 should help the student achieve the following goals:

1. To understand that public speaking has a strong theoretical foundation that has developed in the West over the past two thousand years.

2. To know the leading teachers of rhetorical theory in the West (including Aristotle, Cicero, Quintilian, Blair, Campbell, and Whately) and their major contributions.

3. To become acquainted with key rhetorical terms from the classical period, including logos, ethos, pathos, inventio, dispositio, elocutio, pronuntiatio, and memoria.

4. To have an overview of the development of the study of public speaking in America from colonial times to the twentieth century.

5. To understand why the study and practice of public speaking flourishes in democratic societies.

6. To grasp the ways in which freedom of speech, public speaking, and democracy work together in support of each other and of a free society.

7. To see that the ability to speak well in public serves not only a vocational interest, but also a general citizenship interest in society at large.

Exercises from the Text

1. Aristotle said in the Rhetoric that persuasive speaking had four purposes, namely, (1) to uphold truth and justice, (2) to explain complex matters to ordinary people, (3) to help us understand all sides of an issue and all arguments on that issue, and (4) to defend oneself against unjust accusations. Is this list too limited for today's complex world? What other purposes for persuasive speaking can you add to Aristotle's list?

(<u>Comment</u>. Ask the students to think about Aristotle's list,
then add to it. List the additional purposes of persuasive
speaking on the board as students mention them. Discuss
them in class.)

2. Think for a few moments about the groups,
organizations, and institutions on your college campus, in
your local community, and in the state and nation at large.
Make a list of a dozen or so. How many of those on your
list could function smoothly and effectively if all
informative and persuasive speaking were eliminated?
Narrowing to the college campus, consider how much of your
education--starting with classroom lectures and
discussions--depends on some form of public address.

(<u>Comment</u>. Ask students to bring their written lists to
class. Randomly choose several students to put their lists
on the board. Discuss the way that public speaking is used
in the groups listed. Also, discuss the difficulties that
would occur for the groups if all public speaking were
prohibited.)

Additional Exercises

1. Assign a short paper on "My Future Use of Public
Speaking." Have several students read their papers in
class, and then have an open discussion on the subject. An
optional assignment would be for a short speech on the
subject rather than a written paper.

2. As a part of the lecture material for this
chapter, the instructor could research the way in which the
Greeks or the Romans (or both) governed themselves in their
democratic periods. This should include the specific way in
which the legislature worked, and the way in which the
courts worked. The place of public speaking in the
functioning of Greek or Roman democracy should be
emphasized. For a start, the instructor could consult
Golden, Berquist, and Coleman, pp. 1-15, in the list of
resources below.

3. Chapter 1 points out that Aristotle defined
rhetoric as "the faculty of discovering in the particular
case what are the available means of persuasion." Lead a
class discussion of this definition and its implications for
the study of public speaking.

4. Lead the class in a discussion of this statement
from the "in brief" summary of Chapter 1: ". . . a free
society gives birth to both freedom of speech and the study
and application of the principles of effective public
communication (including public speaking). The three
components--a free society, freedom to speak, and public

communication--nourish one another. When one is missing,
the others are diminished in strength and may wither and
die."

Resources

Aristotle. The Rhetoric of Aristotle. Lane Cooper, tr.
    New York: Appleton-Century, 1932. (Or, use some other
    standard translation, such as that of R. C. Jebb.)

Benson, Thomas W., and Prosser, Michael H., eds. Readings
    in Classical Rhetoric. Boston: Allyn and Bacon, 1969.
    (Reprinted by Hermagoras Press, 1988.)

Bonner, Robert J. Aspects of Athenian Democracy. New York:
    Russell & Russell, 1967 (reprint of the 1933 edition).

Golden, James L., and Corbett, Edward P. J., eds. The
    Rhetoric of Blair, Campbell, and Whately. New York:
    Holt, Rinehart and Winston, 1968.

Golden, James L., Berquist, Goodwin F., and Coleman, William
    E. The Rhetoric of Western Thought, 4th ed. Dubuque,
    Iowa: Kendall/Hunt, 1989.

Kennedy, George. The Art of Persuasion in Greece.
    Princeton: Princeton University Press, 1963.

Kennedy, George. The Art of Rhetoric in the Roman World.
    Princeton: Princeton University Press, 1972.

Tedford, Thomas L. Freedom of Speech in the United States.
    New York: Random House, 1985. Chapter 1, "Freedom of
    Speech: The Classical and English Heritage," and
    Chapter 2, "Freedom of Speech in America to World War
    I."

Thonssen, Lester, Baird, A. Craig, and Braden, Waldo W.
    Speech Criticism, 2nd ed. New York: Ronald Press,
    1970. See especially the historical materials in
    chapters 2 through 7.

Examination Questions

Multiple-Choice

1. Who was the teacher of public speaking in Syracuse in the 5th century B.C. who is described as the first teacher of public speaking in the West?
    a. Aristotle
    b. Corax
    c. Isocrates
    d. Plato
    e. Thrasybulus

2. Who was the author of the important text on public speaking written in Athens about 330 B.C.? (This text remains influential in the study of public speaking today.)
    a. Isocrates
    b. Tisias
    c. Cicero
    d. Aristotle
    e. Pericles

3. What did the Greeks call that form of proof in persuasion that comes from the credibility of the speaker (the impact of the person speaking on the audience)?
    a. mythos
    b. pathos
    c. ethos
    d. logos
    e. inventio

4. According to Aristotle, the speaker who appeals to fear or anger in persuasion is using what type of proof?
    a. unethical
    b. illogical
    c. emotional
    d. ethos
    e. elocutio

5. The earliest known Roman text on public speaking, composed about 90 B.C., is called:
    a. Rhetorica ad Herennium
    b. The Tisian Manual
    c. The Rhetoric
    d. De Inventione
    e. De Oratore

6. The three forms of proof in persuasion identified by
    Aristotle are logical proof, emotional proof, and what
    other?
    a. reasoning
    b. evidence
    c. appeal to patriotism
    d. psychological appeals
    e. ethical proof

7. The Latin canon of rhetoric that concerned finding
    speech content (including proofs useful for persuasion)
    is called:
    a. logos
    b. inventio
    c. elocutio
    d. dispositio
    e. actio

8. What did the Romans call the study of language in
    public speaking?
    a. elocutio
    b. pronuntiatio
    c. actio
    d. iambus
    e. emotional proof

9. The five classical canons of rhetoric are found
    originally in what work?
    a. Rhetoric
    b. Institutes of Oratory
    c. Rhetorica ad Herennium
    d   De Oratore
    e. Phaedrus

10. Lectures on Rhetoric and Belles Lettres, England's most
    popular speech text of the 18th century, was written by
    whom?
    a. Hugh Blair
    b. Robert Ingersoll
    c. Richard Whately
    d. George Campbell
    e. Samuel Newman

11. What English teacher of rhetoric included the social
    sciences (psychology in particular) in the study of
    public speaking?
    a. Hugh Blair
    b. Richard Whately
    c. George Campbell
    d. John Locke
    e. Edmund Burke

12. What English teacher of rhetoric stressed argumentation
    and logical proof in public speaking, thereby
    influencing the teaching of debate in modern times?
    a.   John Witherspoon
    b.   Francis Bacon
    c.   Joseph Priestley
    d.   George Campbell
    e.   Richard Whately

13. Who from the list below was both a teacher of public
    speaking and a President of the United States?
    a.   George Washington
    b.   Thomas Jefferson
    c.   Abraham Lincoln
    d.   John Quincy Adams
    e.   John Witherspoon

14. According to Chapter 1, the teaching of public speaking
    and debate had become a standard part of the curriculum
    in numerous American schools and colleges by when?
    a.   The beginning of the twentieth century
    b.   About 1776
    c.   Around the time of the Civil War
    d.   About 1920, following World War I
    e.   About 1948, following World War II

15. Who was the American teacher of public speaking whose
    1927 edition of Fundamentals of Speech set forth a
    theory of persuasion based on modern behavioral
    psychology?
    a.   James Curlin
    b.   Samuel Newman
    c.   Charles H. Woolbert
    d.   John Adams
    e.   Winan O. James

Short Answer

16. How does Aristotle define rhetoric? (You may quote
    directly, or give an accurate paraphrase.)

17. What are the three elements of ethos, or "ethical
    proof," stated by Aristotle?

18. Define this canon of rhetoric: inventio.

19. Define this canon of rhetoric: dispositio.

20. Define this canon of rhetoric: elocutio.

21. Define this canon of rhetoric: pronuntiatio.

22. Who was the author of the <u>Institutes of Oratory</u> (Rome, 95 A.D.)?

23. Who was the famous Roman orator and statesman who wrote several books on rhetoric, including <u>De Oratore</u>?

24. Name the canon of rhetoric known as the "lost canon," and give at least one reason why this canon is no longer emphasized in the modern speech curriculum.

25. Who were the three outstanding English writers on public speaking in the period of 1750-1850?

Discussion and Essay

26. Explain the circumstances that caused Corax to begin teaching public speaking in ancient Syracuse (5th century B.C.).

27. Aristotle said that there are three forms of proof in persuasion: <u>logos</u>, <u>ethos</u>, and <u>pathos</u>. Explain each of these, then comment on how they work together to form a unified system of persuasion.

28. Discuss and explain the following statement from the conclusion of Chapter 1: "[A] free society gives birth to both freedom of speech and . . . public speaking. The three components--a free society, freedom to speak, and public communication--nourish one another. When one is missing, the others are diminished in strength and may wither and die."

Chapter 2

Your First Speeches

Chapter Goals

The content of Chapter 2 should help the student achieve the following goals:

1. To realize that speech subjects should be appropriate for the speaker, audience, and occasion.

2. To see how broad subjects can be narrowed, then phrased according to a general purpose and a specific purpose into the central idea of the speech.

3. To understand that the points of a speech should be supported with specific speech materials, such as examples, comparison and contrast, statistics, and authoritative statements.

4. To become acquainted with the basic principles of logical outlining.

5. To learn that effective speech delivery includes visual directness, bodily communication, and vocal variety.

6. To learn some basic principles of dealing effectively with speech anxiety (stage fright).

Exercises from the Text

1. The next time you are a member of the audience in a public speaking situation, analyze your personal expectations for the speech or speeches scheduled. Would you describe your expectations as "reasonable, modest, and sympathetic"? If so, is it not safe to assume that others think similarly about you when you are speaking? Apply these thoughts to yourself prior to your next speech.

(Comment. Require the students to attend a campus or community program that features a speaker, and to keep notes on their subjective feelings, expectations, and reactions to the speaker. An alternate approach is to have the students do this in class for a complete round of speeches. Have the reports submitted in writing in brief form. Discuss the results of the assignment in class, with specific application to speech anxiety.)

2. Identify an effective speaker on your campus or in your community. You might choose a teacher, a business or

professional person (such as an attorney), or your minister.
Talk with that person about "stage fright." Does he or she
agree that some prespeech tension is normal, or that
experience in speaking helps reduce tension and nervousness?
What recommendations does this person make to help you
control public speaking anxiety?

(Comment. Require each student to interview one person as
required by this exercise. The results should be submitted
in written form, and discussed in class. An alternative is
to have the results given orally in class as a short
speech.)

Additional Exercises

1.   Prior to delivery of the first speech, lead the
class in a discussion of the model outlines and note cards
in Appendix II of the text. Answer student questions about
course standards for outlines and the use of notes while
speaking. Note one or two of the best student outlines
turned in during this round of speeches. After securing
permission from the students whose outlines you choose, make
copies for the class. Distribute and discuss as a means of
clarifying course standards for outlining.

2.   Ask each student to prepare a brief (one or two
pages) paper on the topic: "My Goals in This Course." Tell
the students to be clear, naming specific problems they want
to overcome and goals they want to achieve. Use the papers
as the basis for a class discussion of individual problems
and goals in public speaking.

3.   Write this statement on the board: "The speaker's
main problem is not stage fright or delivery, but having
something worthwhile to say that he or she really wants to
say." Lead the class in a discussion of this statement.
Use the exercise as a means of emphasizing the importance of
choosing good topics for each speech delivered in the
course.

4.   If videotaping facilities are available, record
the first round (or other early round) of speeches. During
playback, discuss the matter of speaking anxiety in terms of
the material concerning anxiety in Chapter 2. Ask the
students to evaluate whether or not they appear on tape as
"tense" or "anxious" as they felt during delivery. Also,
encourage them to use the playback as a means of building
self-confidence and overcoming speaking anxiety.

Resources

Ayers, Joe. "Perception of Speaking Ability: An
    Explanation for Stage Fright." Communication Education
    35 (July 1986): 275-287.

Daly, John A., et al. "Pre-Performance Concerns Associated
    with Public Speaking Anxiety." Communication Quarterly
    37 (Winter 1989): 39-53.

Faules, Don, Littlejohn, Steve, and Ayres, Joe. "An
    Experimental Study of the Comparative Effects of Three
    Instructional Methods on Speaking Effectiveness."
    Communication Education 21 (January 1972): 46-52.

Fritz, Paul A., and Weaver, Richard L., II. "Teaching
    Critical Thinking Skills in the Public Speaking Course:
    A Liberal Arts Perspective." Communication Education
    35 (April 1986): 174-182.

Furr, H. Bedford. "Influences of a Course in
    Speech-Communication on Certain Aspects of the Self-
    Concept of College Freshmen." Communication Education
    19 (January 1970): 26-31.

McCroskey, James C. "Classroom Consequences of
    Communication Apprehension." Communication Education
    26 (January 1977): 27-33.

Richmond, Virginia P., and McCroskey, James C.
    Communication: Apprehension, Avoidance, and
    Effectiveness, 2nd ed. Scottsdale, Ariz.: Gorsuch
    Scarisbrick, 1989.

Video. "Be Prepared to Speak," 27 minutes. Toastmasters
    International and Kantola/Skeie Productions.
    This program is appropriate for use early in the public
    speaking course. It has three sections: speech
    preparation, speech presentation, and dealing with
    stage fright.

Video. "Stage Fright," 13 minutes. Coronet/MTI
    Film and Video.
    A dramatized presentation of specific techniques for
    controlling stage fright.

Examination Questions

<u>Multiple-Choice</u>

1. Determining the predisposition of listeners to respond
   to your proposals in a favorable or unfavorable way
   involves what element of audience analysis?
   a. audience interests
   b. audience attitudes
   c. audience knowledge
   d. ethos
   e. the specific purpose of the speech

2. If you decide that your speech is "to inform," you have
   determined:
   a. the subject
   b. the general purpose
   c. the specific purpose
   d. the speech pattern
   e. the central idea

3. "To inform the members of my audience about how a
   fluorescent bulb works" is an example of:
   a. broad subject
   b. central idea
   c. problem-solution plan
   d. specific purpose
   e. general purpose

4. When should you use complete sentences in the outline?
   a. for the main points only
   b. for all points
   c. for the points of the body only
   d. for direct quotations only
   e. never use complete sentences in an outline

5. During delivery, the sentence in which you tell the
   audience the purpose of the speech is called the:
   a. narrowed subject
   b. central idea
   c. specific purpose
   d. general purpose
   e. preview of main points

6. If, while speaking, you illustrate a point with a
   story, what type of supporting material are you using?
   a. humor
   b. authoritative statement
   c. literal analogy
   d. direct quotation
   e. specific example

7.　"To persuade" is an example of:
　　a.　audience analysis
　　b.　specific purpose
　　c.　central idea
　　d.　general purpose
　　e.　broad topic

8.　If the main points of a speech on how to make something are organized according to the first step, the second step, the third step, etc., what pattern is being used?
　　a.　chronological
　　b.　topical
　　c.　cause-to-effect
　　d.　effect-to-cause
　　e.　problem-solution

9.　Where should you look while delivering a speech?
　　a.　slightly above the heads of listeners
　　b.　at foreheads or chins of listeners
　　c.　directly into the eyes of listeners
　　d.　at one or two persons whom you know
　　e.　at your notes so you won't lose your place

10.　Which of these does the text recommend as a practical means of controlling speech anxiety:
　　a.　memorize the speech
　　b.　singing lessons
　　c.　walking briskly or jogging before class
　　d.　awareness that all speech anxiety is imaginary
　　e.　thoroughly master speech content

Short Answer

11.　Audience analysis for speechmaking includes three major things, the first being audience interests. What are the other two?

12.　There are four main types of supporting materials for speeches, one of which is statistics. What are the other three?

13.　You should keep the total number of main points of the body of the speech within the range of _____ to _____.

14.　Complete the following statement concerning speech anxiety (you may quote or paraphrase): Fear of public speaking emerges from a personal assessment that:
_____.

15. Complete this second statement concerning speech anxiety (you may quote or paraphrase): Fear of public speaking is intensified when the speaker believes that:_____.

Discussion and Essay

16. Explain the difference between a broad subject and a narrowed subject. Give two <u>original</u> examples that show the movement from broad to narrow, one suitable for an informative speech, and the other suitable for a persuasive speech.

17. Explain specific purpose and central idea, including how they are similar and how they are different. Assuming that both come from the same speech, give an original example of the correct phrasing for a specific purpose and a central idea.

18. State a central idea suitable for a component parts outline, then outline the main points that illustrate the component parts pattern.

19. State a central idea suitable for a topical outline, then outline the main points that illustrate the topical pattern.

20. Summarize and discuss what Chapter 2 says about speech anxiety problems that are primarily "imaginary" and those that are "real."

Chapter 3

Democratic Values, Free Speech, and Speaker Ethics

Chapter Goals

The content of Chapter 3 should help the student achieve the following goals:

1. To become aware of some basic values that support democracy, including respect for individuals, belief in human capacity to reason, and the principle of equality.

2. To grasp the interacting relationship that exists among democratic values, the practice of free speech, and the principles of communication ethics.

3. To learn of the specific constraints that the U.S. Supreme Court has imposed on the practice of free speech in the United States.

4. To think seriously about issues of right and wrong in public speaking, and to begin formulating a personal philosophy of communication ethics.

Exercises from the Text

1. Keep a "Freedom of Speech and Communication Ethics" scrapbook during the course, saving newspaper and magazine stories on issues and cases of free speech and ethics in public communication. Be sure to record the source, date, and page for your clippings as you enter them in your scrapbook. Near the end of the course arrange with the instructor to show your collection to the class, and to discuss your overall reaction to the problems you have noted.

(Comment. This project could be assigned to all students for grading by the instructor at the end of the course. Instructions might include a specific number of stories, and a request that the student include as many public speaking situations as possible. The project could even provide the basis for a classroom speech on one of these topics: "What I learned about freedom of speech" or "What I learned about communication ethics" from stories saved during the term.)

2. Check with the office of student affairs at your school to see what official regulations, if any, are applicable to student, faculty, and visitor freedom of expression on campus. If the regulations are in print, make copies for your public speaking class. Arrange with the

instructor to distribute the material and to discuss the
rules in class.

(<u>Comment</u>. An alternative is for the instructor to secure
the written regulations, making copies for distribution and
discussion in class. The administrative officer in charge
of enforcing the rules could be invited to the class to
explain the regulations, and to participate in a discussion
about them.)

  3. Think about your own standards of communication
ethics, then write a statement setting out the standards of
ethics you should apply to yourself. Date your statement
and save it for future reference (and for revision and
improvement as additional thoughts occur to you).

(<u>Comment</u>. This exercise can be adapted to a speaking
assignment. After a class discussion on speech ethics, ask
each student to prepare a 4 to 5 minute speech on "My
Philosophy of Communication Ethics." Ask each speaker to
include in the conclusion a clear summary of the key points
of the speech. An alternative is to assign this as a
written project.)

Additional Exercises

  1. Point out to the class that granting freedom of
speech for everyone includes giving freedom of speech to
those whose ideas you detest. Lead the class in a
discussion of the question, "Should freedom of speech be
granted to antidemocratic groups and racists, such as
facists or the Ku Klux Klan?"

  2. Invite a teacher of freedom of speech or media
law, or a local attorney, to speak to the class on current
issues of freedom of expression in the United States. Ask
the speaker to include some issues that are directly related
to public speaking. An alternative is to invite a local
member of the American Civil Liberties Union to class to
explain the ACLU's strong defense of the right to speak,
even for racists and antidemocratic groups. Be prepared to
ask some challenging questions.

  3. Lead the class in a discussion of the question,
"Is it ever morally right to tell a lie?" In advance of
this discussion, ask the students to think about the
morality of telling falsehoods in these hypothetical cases:
to comfort a child about a family tragedy; to comfort a
terminally ill person; to deceive an enemy in time of war;
to mislead an assassin who is looking for a friend; to get
people to take an action that will save their lives.

4.   Ask the class to read the "<u>Credo</u> for Free and Responsible Communication in a Democratic Society," that appears in a special box in Chapter 3. The <u>Credo</u> was endorsed by the Speech Communication Association in 1972. Lead the class in a discussion of this statement, paragraph by paragraph.

Resources

Haiman, Franklyn S. <u>Speech and Law in a Free Society</u>. Chicago: University of Chicago Press, 1981.

Haiman, Franklyn S. "Speech Communication: A Radical Doctrine." <u>Central States Speech Journal</u> 34 (Summer 1983): 83-87.

Hanks, William E. "Mass Media and the First Amendment." <u>Communication Education</u> 24 (March 1975): 107-117.

Holsinger, Ralph L. <u>Media Law</u>. New York: Random House, 1987.

Jaksa, James A., and Pritchard, Michael S. <u>Communication Ethics: Methods of Analysis</u>. Belmont, Calif.: Wadsworth, 1988.

Jensen, J. Vernon. "Teaching Ethics in Speech Communication." <u>Communication Education</u> 34 (October 1985): 324-330.

Johannesen, Richard L. <u>Ethics in Human Communication</u>, 3rd ed. Prospect Heights, Ill.: Waveland Press, 1990.

Johannesen, Richard L. "Teaching Ethical Standards for Discourse." <u>Journal of Education</u> 162 (Spring 1980): 5-20.

McGaffey, Ruth. "A Critical Look at the Marketplace of Ideas." <u>Communication Education</u> 21 (March 1972): 115-122.

McGaffey, Ruth. "Freedom of Speech for the Ideas We Hate: Nongovernmental Abridgment of Freedom of Expression." <u>Free Speech Yearbook</u> (1987), Vol. 26. Carbondale, Ill.: Southern Illinois University Press, 1988.

Minnick, Wayne C. <u>The Art of Persuasion</u>, 2nd ed. Boston: Houghton Mifflin, 1968. See Chapter 11, "The Ethics of Persuasion."

Minnick, Wayne C. "Teaching Free and Responsible Speech: A Philosophical View." <u>Free Speech Yearbook</u> (1972). New York: Speech Communication Association, 1973.

47

Nilsen, Thomas R. Ethics of Speech Communication, 2nd ed.
    Indianapolis: Bobbs-Merrill, 1974.

Tedford, Thomas L. Freedom of Speech in the United States.
    New York: Random House, 1985.

Tedford, Thomas L., Makay, John J., and Jamison, David L.
    Perspectives on Freedom of Speech: Selected Essays
    from the Journals of the Speech Communication
    Association. Carbondale, Ill.: Southern Illinois
    University Press, 1987. (Note: In addition to the
    seventeen essays collected here, this volume includes
    two annotated bibliographies, one on freedom of speech,
    and the other on communication ethics.)

Wallace, Karl R. "An Ethical Basis of Communication."
    Speech Teacher 4 (January 1955): 1-9.

Wallace, Karl R. "The Substance of Rhetoric: Good
    Reasons." Quarterly Journal of Speech 49 (October
    1963): 239-249.

Examination Questions

Multiple-Choice

1. Laws used to punish those who criticize the government
    are known as:
    a. slander laws
    b. laws against anger
    c. libel laws
    d. sedition laws
    e. heresy laws

2. Laws used to punish those who criticize or make fun of
    a society's majority religion are known as:
    a. slander laws
    b. blasphemy laws
    c. provocation-to-anger laws
    d. sedition laws
    e. obscenity laws

3. What was the name of the 1969 case concerning a speech
    made by a member of the Ku Klux Klan in which the U.S.
    Supreme Court provided strong protection for anti-
    government speech:
    a. Engel v. Vitale
    b. Vanderbilt v. Illinois
    c. Brandenburg v. Ohio
    d. Ku Klux Klan v. United States
    e. Schenck v. United States

4. What is the term that describes false speech that tends to destroy the good standing and reputation of a person:
   a. defamation
   b. provocation to anger
   c. "fighting words"
   d. sedition
   e. incitement

5. By legal tradition, there are four types of false charges that are automatically libelous; which of these is not one of the four:
   a. a person is diseased
   b. a person is strict and uncompromising
   c. a person is dishonest
   d. a person is immoral
   e. a person is a criminal

6. Which statement best summarizes the rule developed by the U.S. Supreme Court concerning marches and demonstrations:
   a. by majority vote of the city council, marches and demonstrations can be banned
   b. banning a march on a city street requires a unanimous vote of the city council
   c. citizens have the right to march or demonstrate any time they wish and in any nonviolent way they wish, even without a permit
   d. public places must be open for marches and demonstrations, but their use is subject to reasonable regulation
   e. groups may march provided they pay a fee determined by the state legislature

7. Which statement best summarizes the action of the U.S. Supreme Court concerning academic freedom on the college campus:
   a. academic freedom is allowed only for the library
   b. academic freedom is not a constitutional right, but it is a good thing for American education
   c. academic freedom is for students only
   d. academic freedom is protected in private schools, but not in those owned by the state
   e. academic freedom is for teachers, but not for students

8. The "good man theory" of rhetoric was set out by what ancient teacher of rhetoric?
   a. Plato
   b. Quintilian
   c. Aristotle
   d. St. Augustine
   e. Cicero

9. We can trace the origins of democracy and free speech
    in the West to what society:
    a. Egypt
    b. Rome
    c. Greece
    d. England
    e. Holland

10. Chapter 3 urges speakers to choose subjects that meet
    which of these standards:
    a. should always be controversial
    b. should never be controversial
    c. should be based on a belief sincerely held by the
        speaker
    d. should be of interest to the audience, even if not
        sincerely believed by the speaker
    e. speech classes are not real audiences, so it
        doesn't matter what type of subject is used

Short Answer

11. The fundamental values of a democracy include
    individual dignity and worth, plus what two additional
    values?

12. Chapter 3 sets out four assumptions of democracy, the
    first being a preference for persuasion over force.
    What are the other three?

13. In discussing ethics in public speaking, Chapter 3
    urges that the speaker be responsible in four areas of
    communication. The first two are responsibility to
    oneself, and to the audience. What are the other two?

Discussion and Essay

14. Complete the rule on sedition announced by the Supreme
    Court in the Brandenburg case (you may quote, or
    summarize accurately in your own words); then discuss
    and explain its implications for freedom of political
    speech in the United States.

    The Supreme Court said in Brandenburg: "The
    constitutional guarantees of free speech and free press
    do not permit a State to forbid or proscribe advocacy
    of the use of force or of law violation except where
    such advocacy . . . " [complete and explain].

15. Are slander and libel protected forms of expression
    under the First Amendment? Discuss and explain with
    particular application to public speaking.

16.   Summarize and discuss what the U.S. Supreme Court ruled
      about the freedom to criticize religion, based on the
      case of <u>The Miracle</u>, a film banned by the State of New
      York.

Chapter 4

The Communication Process and Listening

Chapter Goals

The content of Chapter 4 should help the student achieve the following goals:

1.   To know how to define "communication."

2.   To know the seven components of the communication process (source, message, channel, receiver, feedback, interference, and situation) and how to define and explain each.

3.   To be able to apply the seven-part communication model to the specific circumstances of speaking in public.

4.   To understand three significant differences between receiving a message by <u>reading</u> and by <u>listening</u>.

5.   To know five basic skills of listening that all persons should develop.

6.   To learn the special skills one should develop for both <u>informational listening</u> and <u>critical listening</u>.

Exercises from the Text

1.   Apply the suggestions of this chapter concerning informational listening to your classes. Use the ideas concerning both mental and written notetaking to evaluate and improve your personal listening skills in the courses you are taking. Make a special effort to improve your method of taking lecture notes.

(<u>Comment</u>. This exercise can be adapted to a round of informative speeches in the public speaking class. Ask each student to listen actively and take notes that include the speaker's central idea, and main points for each speech. Also, ask the students to try to identify which speech pattern is used, such as chronological, component parts, or topical. After the day's informative speeches have been made, and during the instructor's critique, discuss with the class which speeches were the easiest to follow and understand, and why--that is, what specific rhetorical techniques were used to make them clear.)

2.   Attend an event that features a speech on a controversial issue. Using your skills of critical listening, observe whether or not the speaker employs

logical reasoning and sound evidence in support of the
opinions presented. How influential was the speaker's
personality and manner of delivery? Would you classify the
speech as "responsible" or "irresponsible"? What are the
reasons for your classification?

(Comment. This exercise can be assigned as a written report
to be turned in for grading. An alternative is to ask each
student to attend an event as noted above, and to present an
organized oral report to the class about the listening
experience.)

Additional Exercises

1.   Assign the preparation of a simple time schedule for
one day, blocking the schedule into hours, and each hour
into segments of 15 minutes. Ask the students to keep a
speaking-listening diary for one day, jotting down the time
they spend speaking and the time they spend listening.
Discuss the results in class.

2.   Have each student prepare a written list of feedback
and listening behaviors that he or she finds desirable in
others, then evaluate how well he or she applies these
desirable traits in listening to others. The list can come
from both formal (such as public speaking) and informal
(such as conversation) situations. Urge the students to use
this exercise as a means of identifying specific listening
practices of their own that need improvement.

3.   For the instructor who likes to have students study
speech criticism early in the course, Chapter 4 presents a
logical transition point because of the overlap between
critical listening and speech criticism. Assign Appendix I,
"Speech Criticism: Analyzing and Evaluating Public
Speeches." Lead the class in a discussion of Appendix I,
including the relationship of listening to criticism. For
specific exercises, see the unit on Appendix I later in this
manual.

Resources

Berlo, David K. The Process of Communication: An
    Introduction to Theory and Practice. New York: Holt,
    Rinehart and Winston, 1960.

Bostrom, Robert N., and Bryant, Caroll L. "Factors in the
    Retention of Information Presented Orally: The Role of
    Short-Term Listening." Western Journal of Speech
    Communication 44 (Spring 1980): 137-145.

Eisenberg, Abne M. <u>Living Communication</u>. Englewood Cliffs,
    N.J.: Prentice-Hall, 1975.

Fisher, B. Aubrey. <u>Perspectives on Human Communication</u>.
    New York: Macmillan, 1978.

Floyd, James J. <u>Listening: A Practical Approach</u>.
    Glenview, Ill.: Scott, Foresman, 1985.

Nichols, Ralph G., and Stevens, Leonard A. <u>Are You
    Listening</u>? New York: McGraw-Hill, 1957.

Rubin, Rebecca B., and Roberts, Charles V. "A Comparative
    Examination and Analysis of Three Listening Tests."
    <u>Communication Education</u> 36 (April 1987): 142-153.

Steil, Lyman K., Barker, Larry L., and Watson, Kittie W.
    <u>Effective Listening: Key to Your Success</u>. Reading,
    Mass.: Addison-Wesley, 1983.

Stewart, John. "Empathic Listening." <u>Communication
    Education</u> 32 (October 1983): 365-367.

Wolff, Florence I., Marsnik, Nadine C., Tacey, William S.,
    and Nichols, Ralph G. <u>Perceptive Listening</u>. New York:
    Holt, Rinehart and Winston, 1983.

Wolvin, Andrew D., and Coakley, Carolyn G. <u>Listening</u>.
    Dubuque, Iowa: Wm. C. Brown, 1985.

Sound filmstrips. "Receiving a Message, and "Listening and
    Speaking," two filmstrips, each 15 minutes in length.
    Films for the Humanities.
    The filmstrips discuss listening in both informal and
    formal situations. Topics covered include conversation
    analysis, dealing with distractions, and critical
    listening.

Examination Questions

<u>Multiple-Choice</u>

1. According to the communication model explained in
    Chapter 4, the means for conveying a message (such as
    by book, telephone wire, or soundwaves) is called:
    a.   the message
    b.   the resource
    c.   audio-visual aids
    d.   vocal quality
    e.   the channel

2. According to Chapter 4, <u>meaning</u> exists where in public speaking?
   a. good dictionaries
   b. primarily in eye contact
   c. within the members of the audience
   d. primarily in movement and gesture
   e. within the words chosen by the speaker

3. What percentage of communication time is spent in speaking?
   a. 15%
   b. 25%
   c. 40%
   d. 50%
   e. 75%

4. What percentage of communication time is spent in listening?
   a. 15%
   b. 25%
   c. 50%
   d. 60%
   e. 80%

5. As explained in the text, which of these calls for <u>critical</u> listening?
   a. a college lecture
   b. a political campaign speech
   c. a doctor explaining a new medicine
   d. a talk on how to do something
   e. getting directions for going somewhere

6. Studies show that listeners can evaluate a speech how much faster than a speaker can deliver it?
   a. at about the same rate (not much faster)
   b. about 10% faster
   c. about twice as fast
   d. in fact, listeners are slower, not faster
   e. about 3 to 4 times faster

7. If, while listening, you note that the speaker is developing a topic according to a plan of past to present to future, what type of speech pattern is the speaker using?
   a. need-plan-benefits
   b. cause to effect
   c. chronological
   d. topical enumeration
   e. component parts

8. What does the text call the basic listening skill of
    carefully weighing ideas and pausing to think before
    reaching a conclusion:
    a. positive procrastination
    b. negative procrastination
    c. intellectual insulation
    d. critical thinking
    e. postponing decision-making

9. According to the communication model, the <u>channel</u> in a
    public speaking situation is which of these:
    a. voice and body over soundwaves and lightwaves
    b. soundwaves only
    c. lightwaves only
    d. the breath stream
    e. the platform and lectern used by the speaker

10. The speaker who communicates effectively that he or she
    is informed, sincere, and friendly, establishes:
    a. feedback
    b. credibility
    c. pathos
    d. a speech-thought differential
    e. interference insulation

Short Answer

11. Communication can be defined as the process by which
    humans attempt to share <u>thoughts</u>--and what additional
    <u>two</u> things--with one another?

12. According to Chapter 4, words function as symbols and
    do not inject meaning into the minds of the audience.
    Instead, words do what (one sentence)?

13. The communication model outlined in Chapter 4 has seven
    elements, the first being the <u>source</u>. In correct
    order, list the remaining six elements.

Discussion and Essay

14. Explain these three components of the communication
    model: (a) feedback; (b) source; (c) interference.

15. The text explains three ways that receiving a message
    by reading differs from receiving it by listening.
    Name any one of the three and explain it.

16. Explain what is meant by these two listening skills:
    (a) listen past delivery; and (b) use the
    speech-thought differential.

Chapter 5

Analyzing the Audience and Occasion

Chapter Goals

The content of Chapter 5 should help the student achieve the following goals:

1.   To realize the fundamental importance of audience and occasion analysis in speech preparation.

2.   To learn how to gather and use information about the audience and occasion.

3.   To be able to define "attitude," and to know how to apply attitude theory to speech preparation.

4.   To learn specific techniques of speech preparation for the hostile audience.

5.   To know what is meant by audience demographics, and how to apply demographic information to speech preparation.

6.   To know how to analyze the speaking occasion, and how to apply this analysis to speech preparation.

Exercises from the Text

1.   Prior to your next informative speech, prepare and distribute to the class a brief questionnaire designed to find out how much knowledge your classmates have on the subject you plan to discuss. Use the results as a guide in speech preparation (and, if you discover that the audience is generally well informed on the topic, consider changing to another topic about which the audience is less well informed).

(Comment. This exercise can be required for any informative speech in the course. The student could use text Figure 5.2 as a model for the questionnaire, adapting it to the expository presentation.)

2.   Before your next persuasive speech, prepare and distribute to the class an attitudes questionnaire concerning the central idea you plan to support. Use the suggestions in this chapter as a guide to designing a questionnaire that secures information concerning audience attitudes ranging from strong agreement to strong disagreement on your subject.

(<u>Comment</u>. This project could be required for one of the persuasive speeches in the course. The student should be asked to study the chapter carefully, then to use Figure 5.2 as a guide in preparing the attitudes questionnaire. When grading the questionnaire, pay particular attention to the <u>clarity</u> of the questions, and to their <u>relevance</u> to important issues inherent in the speech topic.)

Additional Exercises

1.   Distribute copies of the "Audience Analysis Form" that follows these exercises. Prepare a summary of class demographics based on student responses, and distribute the summary to the class. Discuss how this information can be applied to speech planning in the course.

2.   Make copies of John F. Kennedy's speech on separation of church and state, delivered to the Greater Houston Ministerial Association, September 1960. (The complete speech is reproduced in Part IV of this manual; also, the speech is discussed in Chapter 16 of the text.) Ask the class to study the speech, including the material about it in Chapter 16. Lead the class in a discussion of the speech, with special attention to Kennedy's analysis of both his immediate audience of ministers, and the national audience of voters.

AUDIENCE ANALYSIS FORM
(Class Demographics)

1. Age:_____

2. Sex: ( ) male; ( ) female.

3. Marital status: ( ) single; ( ) married; ( ) separated
   or divorced; ( ) widowed.

4. Religion:_____

5. Racial/ethnic background:_____

6. Political interest and affiliation:

   ( )   unaffiliated; not very interested in politics.

   ( )   I am interested in politics, and am affiliated
         with ( ) Republican Party; ( ) Democratic Party;

         ( ) Other:_____

7. I have lived most of my life in: ( ) rural area;
   ( ) small town under 25,000; ( ) town between 25,000
   and 100,000; ( ) city between 100,000 and 300,000;
   ( ) city above 300,000.

8. My financial support for college: ( ) mainly family;
   ( ) mainly from my own work; ( ) about 50/50 division
   of family and my own work;

   ( ) Other:_____

9. Your college class: ( ) freshman; ( ) sophomore;
   ( ) junior; ( ) senior; ( ) graduate student.

10. Your college major field:_____

11. Career goals:_____

   _____

12. Member of what campus and community organizations:

   _____

   _____

Resources

Andersen, Kenneth E. Persuasion: Theory and Practice, 2nd
    ed. Boston: Allyn and Bacon, 1978. See especially
    Chapters 3 and 4.

Bettinghaus, Erwin P., and Cody, Michael J. Persuasive
    Communication, 4th ed. New York: Holt, Rinehart and
    Winston, 1987. See especially Chapters 2, 3, and 4.

Braden, Waldo W., and Gehring, Mary Louise. Speech
    Practices: A Resource Book for the Student of Public
    Speaking. New York: Harper & Brothers, 1958. Chapter
    4, "The Speaker Meets the Audience," includes several
    case studies of speakers who used careful audience
    analysis to help master difficult speaking situations.

Campbell, Karlyn Kohrs. The Rhetorical Act. Belmont,
    Calif.: Wadsworth, 1982. See Chapter 4, "Obstacles
    Arising from the Audience."

McKinney, Bruce C. "Audience Analysis Exercise." Speech
    Communication Teacher 3 (Winter 1989): 6.

Neumann, David. "Selecting Messages: An Exercise in
    Audience Analysis." Speech Communication Teacher
    4 (Summer 1990): 9.

O'Keefe, Daniel J. Persuasion: Theory and Research.
    Newbury Park, Calif.: Sage Publications, 1990. See
    Chapter 10, "Receiver and Context Factors."

Simons, Herbert W. Persuasion: Understanding, Practice,
    and Analysis, 2nd ed. New York: Random House, 1986.
    See especially Chapters 4 and 8.

Woodward, Gary C., and Denton, Robert E., Jr. Persuasion
    and Influence in American Life. Prospect Heights,
    Ill.: Waveland Press, 1988. See the material on
    audience analysis in Chapter 4, "Social Bases of
    Persuasion."

Zimbardo, Philip G., Ebbesen, Ebbe B., and Maslach,
    Christine. Influencing Attitudes and Changing
    Behavior, 2nd ed. Reading, Mass.: Addison-Wesley,
    1977.

Sound filmstrip. "The Topic and the Audience,"
    15 minutes. Films for the Humanities.
    Summarizes the fundamentals of audience analysis and
    how it influences topic selection and speech purpose.

Examination Questions

Multiple-Choice

1. An analysis of the <u>mental state</u> of the audience should include attitudes, knowledge, and what third area:
    a. I.Q. test scores
    b. family income
    c. religious preferences
    d. audience interests
    e. ethnic background

2. According to Chapter 5, we respond to the events of life in predictable ways because of our:
    a. age
    b. attitudes
    c. emotions
    d. ethos
    e. use of logical reasoning

3. What ancient teacher of persuasion discussed the age of the audience in terms of youth, prime of life, and old age:
    a. Plato
    b. Corax
    c. Aristotle
    d. Tisias
    e. Socrates

4. Modern research reports that a persuasive speech that is two-sided (gives opposing views and answers them) is especially suitable for what type of audience:
    a. male
    b. female
    c. educated
    d. uneducated
    e. farm or rural

5. Which of these is <u>not</u> a type of demographic information:
    a. type of occupation
    b. economic status
    c. group associations
    d. attitude on the subject
    e. ethnic background

6. According to Chapter 5, our attitudes are formed from our:
    a. beliefs and values
    b. beliefs only
    c. values only
    d. emotions
    e. heredity

7. An unstructured question that permits a person to anwer
    in his or her own words is what type of question:
    a.   open-ended
    b.   close-ended
    c.   neutral and useless
    d.   scaled and highly useful
    e.   unbiased

8. Behaviors or goals that we find preferable to their
    opposites (such as honesty is better than dishonesty)
    are called:
    a.   common ground
    b.   values
    c.   attitudes
    d.   beliefs
    e.   comparison and contrast

9. Which of these is specifically recommended as a
    technique for speaking to a hostile audience:
    a.   be very frank and outspoken
    b.   always avoid such situations
    c.   establish rapport and good will
    d.   pretend that you agree with the audience
    e.   begin with evidence proving the audience wrong

10. What type of information does a scaled question reveal
    about the audience:
    a.   attitude on the topic
    b.   level of audience vocabulary
    c.   level of audience intelligence
    d.   average weight of listeners
    e.   key beliefs

Short Answer

11. The text lists five things that you should consider
    when analyzing the occasion, including the nature and
    purpose of the occasion, the overall program, and what
    other three things?

12. There are at least four ways of gathering information
    about the audience and occasion, including general
    observation and use of the library. What are the other
    two ways?

13. State one thing that audience analysis should not do.

Discussion and Essay

14. Define "attitude," then explain how attitude theory can
    be used in audience analysis.

15. Explain what the speaker should do when analyzing the occasion.

16. Explain how demographic information can be used in audience analysis.

17. Explain what is meant by "common ground," and how common ground can be established with an audience.

18. Based on your reading of Chapter 5, what would you advise a speaker to do who was planning to address an audience that was hostile to the central idea of the speech?

Chapter 6

Determining the Subject and Purpose

Chapter Goals

The content of Chapter 6 should help the student achieve the following goals:

1. To learn how to find, choose, and narrow a speech subject.

2. To understand the three general purposes of public speaking, namely, to entertain, to inform, and to persuade.

3. To learn how to formulate the specific purpose of a speech.

4. To learn how to adapt the specific purpose to the audience via the statement of the central idea.

Exercises from the Text

1. During the next round of speeches in your public speaking class, listen carefully for the statement of a central idea by each speaker. Write down the central ideas and note how clear and tactful each was. Could you "improve" upon the way in which certain central ideas were announced? If so, how? Why do you think a change in wording might help?

(Comment. Ask the class to do this assignment for a complete round of speeches. In discussing the central ideas written down, distinguish those that are clear from those not so clear, and make recommendations for improvement where needed. If the speeches were persuasive, discuss which statements were most diplomatic. If any were perceived as too abrupt or undiplomatic, discuss how they might be reworded to get a better reception from the audience.)

2. Make a list of several controversial subjects suitable for speeches. Phrase a specific purpose appropriate to each subject, then, with a familiar audience in mind (such as a club you are in, or your speech class) reformulate each as a diplomatic central idea such as you might employ in announcing your purpose to that audience.

(Comment. For a class project, ask each student to do three adaptations as explained above. Have several students write their subjects and central ideas on the board for discussion by the class.)

3.   Find the central idea for each of the model outlines
and speeches in the appendices to this book. Are any
difficult to find? Are any unclear, or undiplomatic in the
way they are stated? If so, what changes would you
recommend, and why?

(Comment. For this project, ask the students to study the
outlines and speeches in Appendix II, discussing in class
the wording of the central ideas in the two speeches given.
Then, ask the class to locate and write down the central
ideas for the two student speeches in Appendix III. Discuss
the results. Are the central ideas clear? In the case of
the persuasive speech, is the central idea tactfully
phrased?)

Additional Exercises

1.   Early in Chapter 6 the text recommends that students
find subjects both from topical areas and from problem
areas. Using the list of topics under "Subjects Derived
from Topics," and the list of problems under "Subjects
Derived from Problems," ask the students to write each topic
and problem on a note card. Then have them jot down subject
ideas that are suitable for classroom speeches for at least
ten of the topical cards and five of the problem cards. Ask
each student to save the cards for future reference in the
course.

2.   Have a classroom "brainstorming" session concerning
topics and problems of interest to the members of the class
(including campus, community, state, national, and
international topics and problems). Ask the students to put
special "brainstorming energy" to work thinking of subjects
that are worthwhile and current. Assign a student or two to
write the subjects on the board as they are mentioned. Have
the students keep notes on the suggestions as potential
subjects for future speeches.

3.   Assign a careful study of the model outlines and
speeches in Appendix II of the text. Go over the outlines
in this appendix in class, and answer student questions
concerning general purposes, specific purposes, and central
ideas.

Resources

Duffy, Susan. "Using Magazines to Stimulate Topic Choices
     for Speeches." Speech Communication Teacher 1 (Summer
     1987): 2-3.

Fregoe, David H. "Informative vs. Persuasive Speaking: The
     Objects Game." Speech Communication Teacher 3 (Winter
     1989): 13-14.

Grainer, Diane. "Creativity vs. 'My Speech Is About
     Avacados.'" Speech Communication Teacher 4 (Winter
     1990): 14-15.

Glick, I. David. "Tossing LAP'S into Their Laps!" Speech
     Communication Teacher 4 (Winter 1990): 15. Note:
     this exercise is designed to help students find
     subjects for persuasive speeches.

Hugenberg, Lawrence W., and O'Neill, Daniel J. "Speaking on
     Critical Issue Topics in the Public Speaking Course."
     Speech Communication Teacher 2 (Fall 1987): 12-13.

Rowan, Katherine. "The Speech to Explain Difficult Ideas."
     Speech Communication Teacher 4 (Summer 1990): 2-3.

Symposium on Using Common Materials. Communication
     Education 16 (November 1967): 259 ff. Note: this
     symposium provides several articles about having all
     speeches in the course based on a central theme, such
     as "Freedom of Speech."

**Sound filmstrips. "The Topic and the Audience," and "Types
     of Information," each 15 minutes in length. Films for
     the Humanities.**
     The filmstrip on topic and audience, which concerns
     audience analysis and topic selection, is also listed
     as a resource for Chapter 5. The filmstrip on types of
     information helps the student better understand how the
     general purpose "to inform" differs from other general
     purposes.

Examination Questions

Multiple-Choice

1. "Crime in America" is an example of:
    a. general purpose
    b. specific purpose
    c. central idea
    d. broad subject
    e. narrowed subject

2. In Chapter 6, the result of combining the general purpose with a narrowed subject is called the:
    a. crux of the issue
    b. specific purpose
    c. point of disagreement
    d. statement of exposition
    e. title of the speech

3. Which of these is not a type of informative speaking:
    a. speech of exposition
    b. lecture
    c. change-of-behavior speech
    d. how-to-do-it speech
    e. teaching

4. According to Chapter 6, the speech to entertain is:
    a. limited to that which amuses
    b. persuasion presented in an interesting way
    c. information presented in an interesting way
    d. any speech that uses humor extensively
    e. actually not a speech but a stand-up comedy routine

5. "To inform my audience of how a bill becomes law in our state legislature" is an example of:
    a. central idea
    b. general purpose
    c. specific purpose
    d. narrowed subject
    e. broad subject

6. "To persuade my audience to vote for Jim Jones for President of the Student Government Association" is an example of:
    a. central idea
    b. general purpose
    c. specific purpose
    d. narrowed subject
    e. broad subject

7. A speech to persuade:
   a. may include entertaining content, but not informative content
   b. may include both entertaining and informative content
   c. may include informative content, but not entertaining content
   d. should be strictly persuasive, excluding all material to entertain or to inform
   e. must include humor to be effective

8. The sentence in the delivered speech in which the speaker announces the purpose of the speech to the audience is called:
   a. narrowed subject
   b. specific purpose
   c. central idea
   d. general purpose
   e. speech title

9. "Our library should phase out the Dewey Decimal System and adopt the Library of Congress System for cataloging books" is an example of:
   a. central idea of an informative speech
   b. a cause-effect argument
   c. narrowed subject
   d. specific purpose of a persuasive speech
   e. central idea of a persuasive speech

10. "I would like to explain to you the process used by our local blood bank to test the safety of the blood supply" is an example of:
    a. central idea of an informative speech
    b. central idea of a persuasive speech
    c. an informative specific purpose
    d. a persuasive specific purpose
    e. a narrowed speech subject

Short Answer

11. The speech subject should be appropriate to what three things?

12. What are the three general purposes of public speaking?

13. In addition to locating subjects in topics (such as "education"), you can find subjects in:

    _____.

Discussion and Essay

14. Explain the difference between the specific purpose and the central idea of a speech. Illustrate your answer with a good, original example of a specific purpose and a central idea.

15. Explain the differences in speeches to entertain, to inform, and to persuade.

Chapter 7

Supporting Materials for Public Speeches

Chapter Goals

The content of Chapter 7 should help the student achieve the following goals:

1. To know the types of supporting material useful in public speaking.

2. To understand the functions of supporting material.

3. To know the standards that all speech supports should meet, as well as the specific tests that should be applied to each type of support.

4. To understand the three measurements of central tendency (or types of "average") used by statisticians, and which are most useful to the public speaker.

5. To know the different types of visual aids, and when visual aids are needed to support speech content.

6. To learn how to prepare and use visual aids.

Exercises from the Text

1. Read two or more of the model speeches in the appendices. On a piece of paper, note how many of the major types of support—examples, comparison and contrast, statistics, and authoritative statements—you find in each speech. Which types of support appear most often? Which types "grab your attention" most effectively?

(Comment. This exercise can be assigned as a written project to be submitted for grading. The instructor might wish to specify which speeches are to be studied. An alternative is to do this as an in-class exercise, having students identify forms of support in the speeches provided in Appendix II and Appendix III of the text.)

2. Listen to several lectures or speeches while focusing on the specific examples, comparisons and contrasts, statistics, and statements from authority employed by the speaker. Which type of support did you find most interesting? Are general statements clearer and more persuasive when backed up by concrete supports?

(Comment. This exercise could be assigned as a project to be graded, based on listening to a given number of campus lectures and speeches, as determined by the instructor. An alternative is to assign it for a round in the public speaking course, having the students note supporting materials in the speeches of their classmates.)

3.   During the term of your public speaking course, pay particular attention to how your classmates, your professors (in all courses), and other speakers you hear on and off campus make use of visual aids. Make a note of both effective and ineffective uses of visual aids. Based on your observations, compose a list of those things you should do, and those things you should avoid doing, when supporting a speech with visuals.

(Comment. During the round of visual aids speeches in the public speaking class, let students assist the instructor in critiquing visual supports and how they were used. Ask students to jot down specific strong and weak points about the visual aids as they listen. Discuss student observations during the critique period.)

Additional Exercises

1.   Examine the student speech in Part IV of this manual. Note that a space is provided on the left side of the page for comments by the students. Make copies and distribute. Ask the students to study the supporting materials used in the speech, identifying each type of evidence in the comments column. After this has been done, ask that each instance of speech support be evaluated according to the tests that apply, as explained in Chapter 7. The evaluation can be recorded in the comments column using a three-point scale: 1 for below average; 2 for average; and 3 for above average.

2.   Chapter 7 explains that modern photocopying has made the handout (a copy for each person in the audience) a practical medium for displaying visual aids. Assign the students a library project in which they locate page-size diagrams, charts, or maps that explain some complex subject in a clear manner. Have the students make photocopies of their best example for class distribution. Distribute the results in class, letting each student explain briefly why he or she found the diagram, chart, or map to be impressive in communicating knowledge in a clear way.

Resources

Borden, Richard D. Public Speaking--As Listeners Like It!
New York: Harper & Brothers, 1935. See especially
Chapter 2, "Listeners' Laws for Speech Substance."

Braden, Waldo W., and Gehring, Mary Louise. Speech
Practices: A Resource Book for the Student of Public
Speaking. New York: Harper & Brothers, 1958. See
Chapter 5, "The Speaker Supports His Proposition."

Feliciano, Gloria D., Powers, Richard D., and Kearl, Bryant
E. "The Presentation of Statistical Information." AV
Communication Review 11 (May-June 1963): 32-39.

Huff, Darrell. How to Lie with Statistics. New York: W.
W. Norton, 1954.

Lefferts, Robert. Elements of Graphics: How to Prepare
Charts and Graphs for Effective Reports. New York:
Harper & Row, 1981.

Newman, Robert P., and Newman, Dale R. Evidence. New York:
Houghton Mifflin, 1969. Includes chapters on the use
of evidence, choosing credible evidence, and the
special problems of statistical evidence.

Runyon, Richard P. How Numbers Lie: A Consumer's Guide to
the Fine Art of Numerical Deception. Lexington, Mass.:
Lewis, 1981.

Film/Video. "Aids to Speaking." Coronet/MTI Film & Video.
This 15 minute video provides tips on the use of visual
aids (as well as some advice on how to use a microphone
and a lectern).

Sound filmstrips. "Choosing the A-V Dimension," and
"Producing Your Presentation," each filmstrip
15 minutes in length. Films for the Humanities.
These filmstrips concern the preparation and use of
audio-visual materials to enhance a presentation.

Examination Questions

Multiple-Choice

1.   All supporting material should meet what three basic
     standards:
     a.   documented, persuasive, and clear
     b.   accurate, relevant, and clear
     c.   entertaining, persuasive, and clear
     d.   humorous, logical, and accurate
     e.   balance among ethos, pathos, and logos

2. A fictional illustration, made up by the speaker to
    support a point, is called:
    a. unethical support
    b. false anecdote
    c. hypothetical example
    d. comparison and contrast
    e. evidence via pathos

3. A speaker who says that life is like a baseball game,
    with some players striking out and others making home
    runs is using what type of support:
    a. figurative analogy
    b. contrast
    c. literal comparison
    d. alliteration
    e. disjunctive example

4. If you add ten examination scores, then divide the
    result by ten, what do you get:
    a. the median
    b. the percentage
    c. the standard deviation
    d. the mean
    e. the mode

5. The mid-point of a set of numbers arranged according to
    size is called:
    a. the median
    b. the percentage
    c. the standard deviation
    d. the mean
    e. the mode

6. If you quote an experienced commercial pilot on the
    dangers of air-traffic congestion in America's
    airports, what type of support would you be using:
    a. hypothetical example
    b. anecdotal evidence
    c. literal analogy
    d. authoritative statement
    e. parallel case

7. To "qualify your source" of testimony means to:
    a. explain your research technique
    b. explain where material is located in the library
    c. tell audience the qualifications of person
        testifying
    d. explain that you used a personal interview
    e. explain that the experience is not personal, but
        happened to some other person

8. In Chapter 7, which of these is recommended for
    persuasive speaking:
    a.   avoid hypothetical examples
    b.   avoid visual aids
    c.   use several hypothetical examples
    d.   avoid statistics
    e.   avoid using comparison and contrast

9. A comparison is the same thing as:
    a.   analogy
    b.   percentage
    c.   anecdote
    d.   typical example
    e.   cause-to-effect reasoning

10. The "arithmetic mean" is also called:
    a.   a simple average
    b.   the mid-point of a set of numbers
    c.   the most-often-occurring score
    d.   the standard score
    e.   the basic percentile

Short Answer

11. What are the three basic functions of supporting
    materials in a speech?

12. Of the three types of averages (measures of central
    tendency) explained in the text, which is of _least_ use
    to the public speaker?

13. What are the three tests that should be applied to
    examples?

14. What are the two tests that should be applied to
    comparisons and contrasts?

15. What are the three tests that should be applied to
    statistics?

16. What are the three tests that should be applied to
    statements from authority?

Discussion and Essay

17. Explain and give at least one good example of each of
    the four types of supporting material, namely,
    examples, comparison and contrast, statistics, and
    statement from authority.

18. Discuss and explain this statement: "present
    statistics in a form that facilitates understanding."

19. Assume that a person who was planning a speech that included statistical evidence came to you for advice on the best way to use and present statistics in speechmaking. What would you say to that person?

20. Explain what is meant by "qualify your source."

Chapter 8

Research: Finding Speech Materials

Chapter Goals

The content of Chapter 8 should help the student achieve the following goals:

1.   To learn how to use the resources of the library to find speech materials.

2.   To learn how to find speech materials by conducting personal interviews.

3.   To learn how to locate speech materials by personal investigations and by writing to organizations.

4.   To learn how to conduct research in an organized way, and to record the results systematically.

Exercises from the Text

1.   Visit your library and ask for copies of published guides to library usage. Inquire about lectures and guided tours that explain basic research techniques. Sign up for a lecture and tour. Prior to the lecture, study the published guides and prepare a list of questions concerning things you would like to know more about. Keep all information on file for future reference.

(Comment. Arrange for a special library tour for the class. An alternative is for the instructor to take the library tour, securing copies of basic library guides for each member of the class. Based on what was learned during the tour, and from the published guides, the instructor could prepare a lecture on research that is tailored to the institution's library.)

2.   In preparing your next speech for which library research is needed, try the two efficiency techniques recommended in this chapter, namely: reading an overview article in an encyclopedia, and systematically browsing through books on your subject as they are grouped together on the shelves. Apply the same techniques to other research projects (such as term papers) as well, until you develop a personal approach to efficient use of the techniques.

(Comment. For the next classroom speech, ask each student to jot down the topic that he or she plans to talk about. After approving the topics as being suitable for the assignment, ask the students to do the two efficiency techniques described above, keeping a written account of the results. Ask for a brief written report on what was found by searching encyclopedias and by browsing in the stacks.)

Additional Exercises

1.   Many students seem to think that the Readers' Guide to Periodical Literature is the only research tool they need to consult when looking for articles on a speech topic.   To help them learn what help is available in other periodical indexes, assign a written report on the results of checking the subject of the next speech in each of the following: Applied Science and Technology Index; Business Periodicals Index; Education Index; Humanities Index; and Social Sciences Index.   If your library has The Magazine Index, which is on a microfilm reader, add this tool to the list.

2.   Check with the library to find out what newspapers your library keeps, and whether the files are bound or microfilm. Also, get a list of the newspaper indexes available on your campus.   Make copies of the results and distribute to the class.   Assign a research project that requires the students to consult at least two of the newspaper indexes, and at least two different newspapers.

3.   Invite the librarian in charge of computer searches to lecture to the class on what a computer search can and cannot do.   Ask the librarian to bring a copy of a recent search so that students can see the results.   An alternative is for the instructor to gather the material from the librarian, explain to the class the computer search services available locally, and pass around some copies of computer search results.

4.   Ask the students to do at least one interview in preparation for a classroom speech.   They should follow the instructions for interviewing that are given in Chapter 8. When the speeches are delivered, have the students attach to the speech outline a copy of their planning for the interview, the questions asked, and a summary of the notes taken.   Evaluate and grade the interview reports.

5.   Early in the term, ask each student to choose an organization (or a subject for which they can find a related organization) to which they can write for information. Using the Encyclopedia of Associations, or the National Trade and Professional Associations of the United States, have each student write for information.   Announce a date later in the term when all students will bring to class the materials they secured by mail. Discuss the results.

Resources

Berkman, Robert I. Find It Fast: How to Uncover Expert
    Information on Any Subject. New York: Harper & Row,
    1987.

Gates, Jean K. Guide to the Use of Books and Libraries, 5th
    ed. New York: McGraw-Hill, 1983.

Hunt, Gary, and Eadie, William. Interviewing: A
    Communication Approach. New York: Holt, Rinehart and
    Winston, 1987.

Mann, Thomas. A Guide to Library Research Methods. New
    York: Oxford University Press, 1987.

Skopec, Eric W. Situational Interviewing. New York:
    Harper & Row, 1986.

Stewart, Charles J., and Cash, William B., Jr.
    Interviewing: Principles and Practices, 5th ed.
    Dubuque, Iowa: Wm. C. Brown, 1988.

Sound filmstrips. "Planning Your Needs," and "Speakers
    and the Library," both concerning research.
    Also, "Learning from Others," and "Presenting
    Yourself," both conerning interviews. Each
    filmstrip is 15 minutes in length. Films for
    the Humanities.

Examination Questions

Multiple-Choice

1. A systematic way of learning how a subject (such as a
    speech topic) is listed in the card catalog or online
    computerized catalog is to check what reference:
    a.   Index to Vital Speeches of the Day
    b.   Library of Congress Subject Headings
    c.   Readers' Guide to Periodical Literature
    d.   Encyclopedia Americana
    e.   International Topical Index

2. For libraries with an online (computerized) catalog,
    which would you do to find books that have the word
    "censorship" in their titles:
    a.   use the National Key Word Index
    b.   this procedure cannot be done with a computerized
         catalog
    c.   use the Encyclopedia Americana
    d.   do a key word search
    e.   use the International Topical Index

3. To find articles on your speech topic in popular magazines, such as <u>Newsweek</u> or <u>Psychology Today</u>, which research tool would you consult:
   a. the card catalog
   b. <u>Speech Topic Encyclopedia</u>
   c. <u>Readers' Guide to Periodical Literature</u>
   d. <u>Facts on File</u>
   e. <u>Great Magazines of the Western World</u>

4. What research tool pulls together (cumulates) the articles of several newspapers for the preceding three years:
   a. <u>The National Newspaper Index</u>
   b. <u>The New York Times Index</u>
   c. <u>The Washington Post Index</u>
   d. <u>Index of the World Press</u>
   e. <u>Resources for Current Research</u>

5. To find the results of public opinion polls, such as the Harris Poll, go first to what research tool:
   a. the <u>Index of Public Opinion</u>
   b. the card catalog
   c. the newspaper indexes
   d. <u>National Opinion Guide</u>
   e. the <u>Gallup Five Year Guide</u>

6. For a summary of the life of a famous American, consult the:
   a. <u>Dictionary of American Biography</u>
   b. <u>World Biography</u>
   c. <u>Information Please Almanac</u>
   d. <u>Education Index</u>
   e. <u>Guide to Greatness</u>

7. The standard index to documents published by the government is:
   a. <u>Public Opinion Quarterly</u>
   b. <u>Jefferson Catalog</u>
   c. <u>Madison Publications</u>
   d. <u>Monthly Catalog of U.S. Government Publications</u>
   e. <u>Federal Reporter</u>

8. Which of these is a monthly report of a major public opinion polling organization:
   a. the <u>Atlantic Monthly</u>
   b. <u>The Gallup Report</u>
   c. <u>Trends</u>
   d. <u>U.S. News & World Report</u>
   e. <u>U.S. Reports</u>

9. A major and widely used source of statistical
    information is:
    a. Times Atlas of the World
    b. Statistical Encyclopedia
    c. Newsweek
    d. Statistical Abstract of the United States
    e. National Guide to Facts and Figures

10. A source that gives the names and addresses of about
    25,000 organizations (in case you want to write away
    for information) is:
    a. Addresses, Inc.
    b. Facts on File
    c. Encyclopedia of Associations
    d. Who's Who in America
    e. International Handbook of Groups

Short Answer

11. The library system that allows you to get materials
    (such as books) from other libraries is known as:

    _____

12. What do you find in The Essay and General Literature
    Index (be clear and specific)?

13. The self-contained microfilm reader that indexes
    leading magazines and periodicals is called:

    _____

14. What American newspaper has been indexed since 1851?

15. The weekly summary of current events that is cumulated
    and indexed annually is:

    _____

Discussion and Essay

16. Explain a computer search, including what it can do for you, what it cannot do for you, and how you go about doing one.

17. Explain how to prepare for, conduct, and evaluate an interview that you might do to get information on a speech topic.

18. What is meant by "systematic browsing"?

19. The text points out that although encyclopedias should not be your sole or main source of information in researching a speech topic, encyclopedias do serve a legitimate purpose in speech preparation. Explain this "legitimate purpose."

Chapter 9

Introducing Outlining: Three Practical Concepts

Chapter Goals

The content of Chapter 9 should help the student achieve the following goals:

1.   To learn the standard rules of wording and sentence structure for a speech outline.

2.   To understand the concept of the speech unit, and how speech units function as the "building blocks" of a good outline.

3.   To learn the three types of relationships that points in an outline have to each other, and how to test the logic of those relationships.

4.   To understand when two or more subpoints are needed to develop a point in a speech outline.

5.   To learn the two situations when it is logical to support a point with only one subpoint.

Exercises from the Text

1.   Pay special attention to the organization of the classroom lectures and speeches you hear in each of your courses over the next several weeks. Are some teachers more organized than others? Does clear, logical organization in a lecture help you understand the content and take a good set of notes? What do your conclusions say about what you should do in organizing your own speeches?

(Comment. This exercise could be assigned for a written report to be graded. Ask each student to listen to one or more speeches, taking notes on the outline--especially on the central idea and the subordinate speech units that support the central idea. Have the student evaluate the speaker's organization, commenting on strong and weak points.)

2.   Select a model speech from the examples at the end of this book. Locate several speech units in the speech, and outline each unit in rough draft form. For variety, outline at least one large unit and one small unit. You can use Figure 9.2 as a model for your outlines.

(<u>Comment</u>. This exercise will probably work best with the student speeches in Appendix III of the text. Assign one or both for students to study and outline.)

3.   Write down two or three topics about which you have strong opinions, then formulate each topic into a specific purpose and central idea for a speech. For each central idea, state the <u>one</u> reason that you believe would be most persuasive in convincing your speech class (or other specific audience) to agree with you. The result, of course, is the basic plan for a one point speech. Could you make a convincing case for any of the topics by developing one, and only one, argument?

(<u>Comment</u>. This exercise could be assigned for grading. Make the number of topics definite, and have the students develop each onepoint speech in outline form. After each onepoint outline, the student should discuss whether or not the argument can be made convincing with this one point. In other words, in this case, is one good reason adequate?)

Additional Exercises

1.   Assign a onepoint persuasive speech for classroom delivery. The students should outline the speech fully, just as they usually do, except that the body of the speech has only one main point with its support. When making the assignment, emphasize the importance of choosing the best argument available for presentation to the class.

2.   Ask each student to photocopy one of the model outlines in Appendix II of the text. Have the students use a pencil to draw a box around each speech unit in the outline, beginning with the body as a whole, and working down to the smallest unit. Discuss the result in class. During the discussion, Exercise 3 below can be applied to the outlines in Appendix II.

3.   In order to help the students understand how to use the "for" test and the "also" test, go over Figure 9.1 in class, calling on various students to orally test from the central idea to the main points, then from the main points on down to the smallest speech unit of that point. To check logical subordination, the student called on should read the superior point <u>aloud</u>, say "for," then read the first subpoint, and on down the line. To check logical coordination, the student should read the first point of a set of coordinate points <u>aloud</u>, say "also," then read the next coordinate point, and on to the end of the set. As noted in Exercise 2 above, this practical exercise can also be done using the model outlines in Appendix II of the text.

Resources

Brown, Kevin J. "'Spidergrams': An Aid for Teaching
    Outlining and Organization." Speech Communication
    Teacher 4 (Spring 1990): 4-5.

Callaghan, J. Calvin. "Testing the Ability to Organize
    Ideas." Communication Education 13 (September 1964):
    225-227.

Hanna, Michael. "Programmed Instruction of the Organization
    of Ideas in the Basic Speech Communication Course."
    Communication Quarterly 22 (Spring 1975): 5-10.

Mills, Glen E. Message Preparation: Analysis and
    Structure. Indianapolis: Bobbs-Merrill, 1966. See
    especially Chapter 5.

Walter, Otis M. Speaking to Inform and Persuade, 2nd ed.
    New York: Macmillan, 1982. See especially Chapters 2
    and 6.

Examination Questions

Multiple-Choice

1.   In the classical canons of rhetoric, what did the
     Romans call the art of speech organization?
     a.   rhetorica ad herennium
     b.   logos
     c.   inventio
     d.   elocutio
     e.   dispositio

2.   What are the two parts of a speech unit?
     a.   an introduction and a conclusion
     b.   a statement and support for that statement
     c.   a problem followed by a solution
     d.   any two points that are coordinate to each other
     e.   a general purpose and a specific purpose

3.   According to the standard rules of outlining, how many
     key ideas can be stated in a single point?
     a.   only one
     b.   two is about right
     c.   three at the most
     d.   five at the most
     e.   there is no limit, provided the ideas are relevant

4. According to Chapter 9, what is the largest and most complete speech unit of a thorough speech outline:
    a. the entire outline, including introduction, body, and conclusion, is one giant speech unit
    b. the first main point of the body
    c. the body of the speech
    d. the introduction
    e. the conclusion

5. The main points of the body of an outline have what logical relationship to the central idea?
    a. they are subordinate
    b. they are coordinate
    c. they are parallel
    d. they are superior
    e. they have no direct logical relationship

6. According to Chapter 9, the "building blocks" of a logical speech outline are called:
    a. main points
    b. speech units
    c. subpoints
    d. general statements
    e. specific purpose and central idea

7. In a speech outline, a point that is directly above some other point (such as point I is above point A) is called:
    a. a main point
    b. a superior point
    c. a building block
    d. a subordinate point
    e. a coordinate point

8. To test the logic of the relationship of main point I to subpoint A in an outline, you should use:
    a. parallel sentence structure
    b. the superiority rule
    c. the one-point-is-enough test
    d. the "for" test
    e. the "also" test

9. To check the way in which all main points of the body (such as points I, II, and III) work together in support of the bigger point above them, you should use:
    a. reasoning by analogy
    b. the triad test
    c. the "for" test
    d. the "also" test
    e. the inventio rule

10. According to Chapter 9, when is it logical to have one, and only one, point of support for a key statement:
    a. when you are using visual aids
    b. when an uninformed speaker knows only one point
    c. when speaking time is short in a persuasive speaking situation
    d. this is never logical, for if you have one point you always must have at least two
    e. only in the introduction when catching attention

Short Answer

11. Complete this sentence: "one of the standard rules of outlining is that each point should be stated as

    _____."

12. The main points of the body actually function as

    _____ that support the central idea.

13. What are the two parts of a speech unit?

    a._____

    b._____

14. A set of two or more subpoints that are equal in that they support the same superior point have what logical relationship to each other? (One word will do.)

Discussion and Essay

15. Explain the concept of the speech unit, and give two or three good examples to illustrate your answer.

16. Explain this statement, and give two or three good examples to illustrate your answer: "a speech has one and only one main point, and that is the central idea."

17. Explain the purpose of the "for" test and the "also" test. Using examples, show how to do both tests.

18. When is it logical to have only <u>one</u> subordinate point of support for a superior point? Explain why it is logical to do this at times. Include examples.

Chapter 10

Organizing and Outlining the Body of the Speech

Chapter Goals

The content of Chapter 10 should help the student achieve the following goals:

1. To learn standard outline form.

2. To understand the basic purpose of a logical speech outline.

3. To know the various speech patterns and how to use them in speech outlining.

4. To understand the fundamental difference between the function of main points in a speech to inform and in a speech to persuade.

5. To become acquainted with Monroe's motivated sequence, and to see where it fits in the scheme of patterns for persuasive speeches.

6. To learn how to support main points with subpoints.

Exercises from the Text

1.   Attend a campus or community program that features a speaker. Listen closely to the speaker's organization, paying special attention to the body of the speech. Can you identify the central idea? Are the main points of the body clearly stated? Is a consistent pattern of organization discernible? What, if anything, could the speaker do to improve the organization of the speech?

(Comment. This exercise can be assigned as a written project to be graded. The student should take notes concerning the clarity of the central idea and main points, and the consistency of the pattern followed by the main points. This can be followed by a brief critique of the strong and weak points of the speaker's organization.)

2.   Browse through a recent issue of Vital Speeches of the Day in your school library. Select a speech that attracts your attention and read it through with a focus on organization. Does the speaker make the central idea clear? Are main points and a pattern of organization obvious to you, or must you reread the speech to locate important headings? Looking further through the issue, do you find that some speeches are better organized than others? Are

those with clear organization easier to read and comprehend?
What lessons concerning the organization of your own
speeches do you get by examining the speeches of others?

(<u>Comment</u>. This exercise can be assigned as a written
project to be graded. An alternative is to assign a speech
or two from Appendix III of the text, or to duplicate and
distribute one of the student speeches in Part IV of this
manual. Have the students outline the assigned speech, and
identify the speech pattern used.)

3.   The next time you make a persuasive speech outside of
class, employ Monroe's "motivated sequence" as the basic
plan for the speech. Study the motivated sequence before
doing this by reading in your library from one of the
editions of Monroe's <u>Principles and Types of Speech</u> (or see
Ehninger, Gronbeck, McKerrow, and Monroe in the reading list
for the chapter). Does the sequence "work well" for you?
Do your listeners seem to follow the movement of your ideas
easily? Was your speech effective?

(<u>Comment</u>. A speech using the motivated sequence can be
assigned for classroom delivery as one of the major
persuasive speeches of the course. If this is done, keep in
mind that Part II of this manual includes a critique form
specifically designed for use in evaluating a talk using
Monroe's plan.)

Additional Exercises

1.   Go over Figure 10.1, the skeleton outline of standard
form, in class. Then move directly to a discussion of the
model outline on "The 'Fair Use' of Copyrighted Material"
near the end of the chapter. Use this discussion to clarify
the standards of outlining for the course, and to answer
student questions about outlining form.

2.   Ask students to make three "skeleton" outlines of
informative speeches using these three patterns:
<u>chronological</u>, <u>physical components</u>, and <u>topical</u>. Then have
the students make three "skeleton" outlines of **persuasive**
speeches using the same three patterns. Discuss in class
the basic difference in function of the main points for the
informative and the persuasive outlines, even though they
use the same patterns. (For this exercise, a "skeleton"
outline consists of a central idea and a set of main points
for the body of the speech. No subpoints are needed, and
the introduction and conclusion are omitted.)

3.   To help students grasp the logical difference between
the function of points in a speech to inform and the
function of points in a speech to persuade, discuss Figure

10.2 in class. This can be combined with the written
assignment explained in Exercise 2 above.

Resources

Andersen, Kenneth E. Persuasion: Theory and Practice, 2nd
     ed. Boston: Allyn and Bacon, 1978. See especially
     Chapter 8.

Braden, Waldo W., and Mary Louise Gehring. Speech
     Practices: A Resource Book for the Student of Public
     Speaking. New York: Harper & Brothers, 1958. Chapter
     3 includes exercises on speech organization; a speech
     using the motivated sequence appears on pp. 33-34.

Campbell, Karlyn Kohrs. The Rhetorical Act. Belmont,
     Calif.: Wadsworth, 1982. See especially Chapter 10.

Ehninger, Douglas, Gronbeck, Bruce E., McKerrow, Ray E., and
     Monroe, Alan H. Principles and Types of Speech
     Communication, 10th ed. Glenview, Ill.: Scott,
     Foresman, 1986. For a discussion of the motivated
     sequence, see especially Chapters 8, 9, and 17.

Sharp, Harry, Jr., and McClung, Thomas. "Effect of
     Organization on the Speaker's Ethos." Speech
     Monographs 33 (June 1966): 182-183.

Thompson, Ernest C. "An Experimental Investigation of the
     Relative Effectiveness of Organizational Structure in
     Oral Communication." Southern Speech Journal 26 (Fall
     1960): 59-69.

Wilson, John F., Arnold, Carroll C., and Wertheimer, Molly
     M. Public Speaking as a Liberal Art, 6th ed. Boston:
     Allyn and Bacon, 1990. See especially Chapters 7 and
     8.

Sound filmstrip. "The Outline," a 15 minute filmstrip.
     Films for the Humanities.
     This filmstrip discusses outlining the introduction,
     body, and conclusion of a speech, balance and
     proportion in the parts of a speech, transitions, and
     speech summaries.

Examination Questions

Multiple-Choice

1. According to Chapter 10, how many main points should
    you have in the body of your speech outline?
    a. one to three
    b. two to five
    c. three to six
    d. between two and ten
    e. never more than three

2. If a speaker explains a college drama program according
    to three main points, namely, the childrens' theater,
    the laboratory theater, and the main stage productions,
    what speech pattern has that speaker used?
    a. chronological
    b. component parts
    c. topical
    d. motivated sequence
    e. from cause to effect

3. If you explain how to make something according to the
    first step of the process, the second step, the third
    step, and so on, what speech pattern have you used?
    a. chronological
    b. component parts
    c. topics inherent in the subject
    d. creative topics
    e. motivated sequence

4. A lecture on the human ear that follows three main
    points, namely, the outer ear, the middle ear, and the
    inner ear, uses what speech pattern?
    a. topics inherent in the subject
    b. creative topics
    c. component parts
    d. motivated sequence
    e. a one-two-three plan

5. A threepoint speech about the federal government based
    on the three branches (legislative, executive,
    judicial) is using what speech pattern?
    a. chronological
    b. component parts
    c. topics inherent in the subject
    d. creative topics
    e. motivated sequence

6. A speech organized around the five steps of attention, need, satisfaction, visualization, and action is following what plan?
   a. basically, it is theory-practice
   b. a complex variation of topical
   c. component parts
   d. the motivated sequence
   e. logical-psychological

7. In a speech to persuade the unique function of the main points is to:
   a. state key reasons
   b. make things doubly clear
   c. hold audience attention
   d. state powerful evidence
   e. appeal for specific action

8. If the economic trends in your state are explained according to trends in the north, central, and south of the state, what speech pattern is being used?
   a. component parts
   b. chronological
   c. inherent topics
   d. creative topics
   e. combination of chronological and topical

9. Monroe's motivated sequence is described in Chapter 10 as an elaborate variation of what basic speech plan?
   a. theory-practice
   b. cause-effect
   c. effect to cause
   d. problem-solution
   e. topical arrangement

10. The term "speech materials" means the same thing as what other term?
    a. main points
    b. subarguments
    c. evidence
    d. burden of proof
    e. pathos

Short Answer

11. What is the goal of the speech to inform?

12. What is the goal of the speech to persuade?

13. What is the function of substatements (subpoints under main points) in the outline of an informative speech?

14. What is the function of substatements (subpoints under main points) in the outline of a persuasive speech?

Discussion and Essay

15. Explain <u>how</u> and <u>why</u> the main points of a persuasive speech and those of an informative speech differ in their function. Illustrate your answer with original examples.

16. List the five steps of Monroe's motivated sequence in correct order, then explain each step clearly.

17. Chapter 10 discusses topics that are inherent in a subject, and topics that are created by the speaker. Explain and give some original examples of inherent topics and creative topics.

18. What is meant by using a <u>climax order</u> and an <u>anticlimax order</u> in a speech outline?

Chapter 11

Introductions, Conclusions, and Transitions

Chapter Goals

The content of Chapter 11 should help the student achieve the following goals:

1. To learn how to plan effective introductions and conclusions for public speeches.

2. To understand the special problems of introductions and conclusions to persuasive speeches, and to the specific ways of dealing with those problems.

3. To learn how to use verbal transitions in public speaking in order to move smoothly from point to point as the speech is delivered.

4. To learn the technique of using "verbal signposts" to help listeners identify important points in a speech.

Exercises from the Text

1. During the next round or two of classroom speeches, take notes on the methods used by your classmates to introduce and to conclude their speeches. What types of introductions and conclusions were used most often? In your opinion, what types of introductions and conclusions were most effective in achieving their respective goals? What do your findings suggest about how you can improve the planning of introductions and conclusions for your own speeches?

(Comment. This exercise can be assigned for a round of speeches. Ask the students to take notes on how each speech is introduced and concluded. Have each student tabulate the results, then write a brief evaluation on the types of introductions and conclusions that were the most effective, and those that were least effective. On the day the assignment is to be turned in, have several students report their findings in class. Discuss the results.)

2. Secure a recent issue of Vital Speeches of the Day in your school library. Note the method of introduction, and the method of conclusion, for each speech in the issue. What type of introduction catches your attention and interest best? Were the conclusions well developed with summaries and clear appeals for belief or action?

(Comment. A variation of this exercise is for the instructor to assign an analysis of the introductions and conclusions of specified speeches in Appendix II or Appendix III of the text.)

3.   Carefully read two or three complete speeches in <u>Vital Speeches of the Day</u>, or from the appendices in this text, paying close attention to the transitions used by the speakers. Select the best speech, photocopy it, and underline each transition word, phrase, and sentence. Notice how "rough" the connection between and among ideas would be if these transitions were deleted.

(<u>Comment</u>. The instructor could specify a speech or two in the appendices of the text for this project. An alternative is for the instructor to make photocopies of a speech, distribute in class, and assign the underlining of transitions as a class project. Perhaps one of the speeches in Part IV of this manual would fit this assignment.)

Additional Exercises

1.   Give each student in the class a copy of the student speech from Part IV of this instructor's manual. Have the students identify the introduction and conclusion of the speech, evaluating each in the comments column to the left. Also, ask that each transition word, phrase, or sentence be underlined throughout the entire speech. If any transitions serve as oral signposts, ask that they be marked with "SP" for "signpost."

2.   Have the students read the two student speeches in Appendix II and the two student speeches in Appendix III of the text, focusing on the specific techniques used by each speaker in the introduction and the conclusion. Lead a class discussion on the assignment, first analyzing the introductions (how the speakers caught attention, established credibility, and won an intelligent hearing), then analyzing the conclusions (how the speakers summarized important points and "wrapped things up" with a creative ending). For the two persuasive speeches, discuss how persuasively (tactfully, diplomatically) the student speakers announced the central idea of the speech, and how effective they were in appealing for belief and/or action in the conclusion.

Resources

Baird, John E., Jr. "The Effects of Speech Summaries Upon Audience Comprehension of Expository Speeches of Varying Quality and Complexity." <u>Central States Speech Journal</u> 25 (Summer 1974): 119-127.

Gregory, Hamilton. Public Speaking for College and Career, 2nd ed. New York: McGraw-Hill, 1990. See especially Chapter 10 on introductions and conclusions.

Gruner, Charles R. "Advice to the Beginning Speaker on Using Humor--What the Research Tells Us." Communication Education 34 (April 1985): 142-147.

McCroskey, James C. An Introduction to Rhetorical Communication, 4th ed. Englewood Cliffs, N.J.: Prentice-Hall, 1982. See especially Chapter 12 on strategies for beginning and ending a speech.

Mills, Glen E. Message Preparation: Analysis and Structure. Indianapolis: Bobbs-Merrill, 1966. See especially Chapter 8 on introductions, conclusions, and transitions.

Examination Questions

Multiple-Choice

1. Considering the speech as a whole, approximately how long should an introduction be?
   a. about 5% of the speech
   b. about 10% of the speech
   c. about 20% of the speech
   d. about 25% of the speech
   e. about 50% of the speech

2. Considering the speech as a whole, approximately how long should a conclusion be?
   a. between 5% and 10% of the speech
   b. at least 12% of the speech
   c. about 20% of the speech
   d. about 25% of the speech
   e. between 25% and 35% of the speech

3. What does the term "rhetorical question" mean?
   a. any question asked in a persuasive speech
   b. a question asked by a listener about the speaker's goal in the speech
   c. a question to which the answer is obvious
   d. a question about the ethics of the speaker
   e. any examination question in a public speaking course

4. In the field of rhetoric, the term ethos means what?
   a. the use of logical argument
   b. the failure to use logical argument
   c. the use of strong evidence
   d. to appeal to audience emotions
   e. speaker credibility with the audience

5. Where should you locate the central idea in a persuasive speech?
   a. always put it in the introduction
   b. for persuasion, never put it in the introduction
   c. place it where it will be most effective
   d. always place it at the end of the conclusion
   e. always put it after main point one of the body

6. The conclusion should have two major goals, the first being to focus on the key points of the speech. What is the second major goal?
   a. giving the final, best argument of the speech
   b. explaining the solution to the problem
   c. explaining the benefits from the solution
   d. visualization
   e. ending the speech in a creative way

7. To move smoothly from point to point in a speech, the speaker should make skillful use of:
   a. humor
   b. preludes and interludes
   c. rhetorical questions
   d. anecdotes
   e. transitions

8. Which of these is not a goal of the introduction of a speech:
   a. catch audience attention
   b. state the key argument and prove it
   c. establish speaker credibility
   d. win an intelligent hearing
   e. gain audience interest

9. If you identify points while speaking by saying "the first point is," "the second point is," and so forth, you are using:
   a. redundancy
   b. alliteration
   c. verbal signposts
   d. rhetorical watering holes
   e. metaphors

10. The speaker who communicates to the audience that he or she is well informed on the subject is helping to establish:
    a. pathos
    b. ethos
    c. logos
    d. inventio
    e. elocutio

Short Answer

11. What are the three primary goals of an introduction?

12. What are the two primary goals of a conclusion?

13. What are the two main functions of transitions?

Discussion and Essay

14. Discuss the special problems (including what you can do about them) of preparing introductions to <u>persuasive</u> speeches, especially when the speech topic is controversial.

15. Discuss the special problems (including what you can do about them) of preparing conclusions for <u>persuasive</u> speeches.

16. What is meant by "end the speech with a creative finishing touch?" Explain, and include some specific ways of accomplishing this "finishing touch."

Chapter 12

Language in Public Speaking

Chapter Goals

The content of Chapter 12 should help the student achieve
the following goals:

1.   To know both the semantic and the stylistic functions
      of language in public speaking.

2.   To understand that just as a map is not the same as the
      territory it represents, a word is not the same as its
      referent.

3.   To realize that, rather than "inject" meaning, words
      stir up meaning already present in the minds of
      listeners.

4.   To understand that effective style in public speaking
      means using language that is appropriate, clear, and
      vivid.

5.   To learn specific ways of improving speaking style,
      including the use of figures of speech.

Exercises from the Text

1.   Using the model speeches in Appendix III, study the
style of Franklin Roosevelt's Declaration of War Address,
John F. Kennedy's Inaugural Address, and Martin Luther
King's "I Have a Dream." Note in particular the use of
figures of speech, including simile, metaphor, repetition,
and antithesis. In the future, and for appropriate
audiences and occasions, employ some of the stylistic
techniques of these great speakers in your own speeches.

(Comment. This exercise can be assigned as a written
project. Using the speeches in text Appendix III, ask each
student to find one or two good examples of simile,
metaphor, repetition, and antithesis, writing them down in
full, and submitting the result for grading.)

2.   While preparing your next persuasive speech, select a
key argument or an important section (such as the
conclusion) for special stylistic enhancement. Write out
the section in full, then revise what you have written,
focusing on making it more colorful and lively with vivid
words and figures of speech. Incorporate your work into the
rehearsal and delivery of the speech. Over time, keep
working on your speaking style until you begin to feel that

clarity and vividness are becoming a more natural part of your preparation and delivery.

(Comment. This exercise can be made concrete by requiring each student to write out a section of the next persuasive speech, deliberately using one or more figures of speech in this written section. Delivery of the written section can be either extemporaneous or read word for word. The student should label the figure or figures used, and submit the written section for grading by the instructor.)

Additional Exercises

1.   Assign a specific speech from Appendix III in the text, or distribute copies of John F. Kennedy's speech to the Houston ministers (see Part IV of this manual). Ask each student to mark and correctly label each figure of speech used by the speaker. Use the project as a basis for a class discussion on speaking style, including the elements of appropriateness, clarity, and vividness.

2.   For the next round of student speeches, ask those in the audience to write down the words and phrases they did not understand, keeping each list by speaker on a separate sheet of paper. At the end of each day's speeches, let students mention some of the words and phrases on their lists. After discussion, the lists can be given to the respective speakers for use in self-improvement.

Resources

Alexander, Hubert G. Meaning in Language. Glenview, Ill.: Scott, Foresman, 1969.

Blankenship, Jane. A Sense of Style: An Introduction to Style for the Public Speaker. Belmont, Calif.: Dickenson Publishing Co., 1968.

Braden, Waldo W., and Gehring, Mary Louise. Speech Practices: A Resource Book for the Student of Public Speaking. New York: Harper & Brothers, 1958. See Chapter 6 on speaking style for a variety of specific examples.

Dieterich, Daniel, ed. Teaching About Doublespeak. Urbana, Ill.: National Council of Teachers of English, 1976.

Einhorn, Lois. "Oral Style and Written Style: An Examination of Differences." Southern Speech Communication Journal 43 (Spring 1978): 302-311.

Harte, Thomas B., Keefe, Carolyn, and Derryberry, Bob R. The Complete Book of Speechwriting for Students and Professionals, 2nd ed. Edina, Minn.: Bellwether Press, 1988. See especially Chapters 9 and 10 on language.

Hochel, Sandra. "Language Awareness and Assessment." Speech Communication Teacher 4 (Winter 1990): 4-5.

Jensen, Marvin D. "Revising Speech Style." Speech Communication Teacher 2 (Summer 1988): 3-4.

Lamoureux, Edward Lee. "Practicing Creative Word Choice with Dialogic Listening." Speech Communication Teacher 4 (Summer 1990): 4-5.

Lee, Irving J. Language Habits in Human Affairs: An Introduction to General Semantics. New York: Harper & Row, 1941.

Rank, Hugh, ed. Language and Public Policy. Urbana, Ill.: National Council of Teachers of English, 1974. Another volume concerned with the problem of doublespeak.

Wilson, John F., Arnold, Carroll C., and Wertheimer, Molly M. Public Speaking as a Liberal Art, 6th ed. Boston: Allyn and Bacon, 1990. See Chapter 9, "Style."

Video. "American Tongues," available in either a 56 minute standard version, or a 40 minute shorter version. The Center for New American Media.
This educational video focuses on linguistic variety in America, and our attitudes toward different dialects and linguistic communities.

Sound filmstrips. "Words and Meaning," and "Style in Language," two 15 minute filmstrips. Films for the Humanities.
These filmstrips discuss how words communicate meaning, the importance of context, choosing the "right" word, and stylistic elements such as appropriateness and clarity.

Examination Questions

Multiple-Choice

1. According to semanticists, the actual thing that a word stands for is called:
   a. the symbol
   b. the inference
   c. an abstraction
   d. the referent
   e. a map

2. The two key functions of language in speechmaking are:
   a. stylistic and semantic
   b. theoretical and practical
   c. abstract and concrete
   d. attention and interest
   e. induction and deduction

3. Words serve to stir up meaning already present in:
   a. society at large
   b. the mind of the listener
   c. the dictionary
   d. the mind of the speaker
   e. the communication channel

4. According to Chapter 12, just as a word is not the thing, a map is not the:
   a. symbol
   b. induction
   c. territory
   d. substitute stimulus
   e. deduction

5. The language of a public speech should be appropriate to:
   a. general purpose
   b. both the general and specific purposes
   c. the speaker, audience, and occasion
   d. current dictionary usage
   e. always make the audience change its mind

6. To "talk the language of your listeners" means to use words that are:
   a. impelling
   b. vivid
   c. wholesome
   d. figurative
   e. familiar

7. To describe a pencil as a "portable hand-held communications inscriber" is to use:
   a. alliteration
   b. doublespeak
   c. simile
   d. alliteration
   e. personification

8. A direct comparison, such as "my Mother is like a beautiful rose," is called:
   a. simile
   b. metaphor
   c. literal analogy
   d. irony
   e. antithesis

9. Patrick Henry's famous words, "Give me liberty or give me death," illustrate what stylistic device:
   a. simile
   b. metaphor
   c. irony
   d. alliteration
   e. antithesis

10. To say that "witchcraft woos to wantonness with wicked words" is to use what stylistic device:
    a. slang
    b. metaphor
    c. simile
    d. alliteration
    e. antithesis

Short Answer

11. If words do not "literally transfer meaning from one person to another," what, according to semantics, do they do?

12. The three elements of style of particular concern to the public speaker are:

    _____, _____, and _____.

13. Complete this definition: "Communication can be defined as the process by which humans attempt to:

    _____.

Discussion and Essay

14. From a semantic standpoint, explain and discuss the implications of this statement for the public speaker: "Just as the map is not the territory, the word is not the thing."

15. From a semantic standpoint, explain and discuss the implications of this statement for the public speaker: "No two people use language in exactly the same way."

16. What is meant by "sexist language"? Give some examples, and explain some specific ways of avoiding sexist language in speaking.

17. Explain "vividness" in language, give some examples, and discuss how to achieve vividness in public speaking.

Chapter 13

Delivering the Speech

Chapter Goals

The content of Chapter 13 should help the student achieve
the following goals:

1.   To know the four types of speech presentation, with
     special attention to the techniques of extemporaneous
     speaking.

2.   To know the characteristics of effective speech
     delivery.

3.   To understand the vocal aspects of delivery, including
     voice, articulation, and pronunciation.

4.   To understand the physical aspects of delivery,
     including physical appearance, facial expression,
     visual directness, posture, movement, and gesture.

Exercises from the Text

1.   Prepare a list of words that you have difficulty
pronouncing, then look up each one in a good, current
dictionary, practicing the standard pronunciation until you
master it. Keep adding to the list during the school year
as other words occur to you.

(Comment. A short starter list is provided the student at
the conclusion of this exercise in the text. The instructor
could prepare an additional list of words that he or she
thinks students in the class need to work on. Students
might be asked to look up the pronunciation of the words on
the list provided by the instructor, writing the dictionary
pronunciation symbols next to each word.)

2.   Rehearse your next speech using a tape recorder. Begin
by deliberately speaking a portion of the speech with a
dull, unexpressive voice. Then start over, speaking the
entire speech with an expressive voice--that is, giving
emphasis and interpretation to the content with variations
of loudness, rate, and pitch. Compare the two types of
vocal technique during playback.

(Comment. This exercise can be done as an in-class project.
The instructor could assign short speech segments from the
model speeches in Appendix II or Appendix III in the text.
Ask the student to read the assigned segment aloud in a

dull, unexpressive voice, then to reread the segment aloud
using vocal variety and an expressive voice.)

3. If you have access to a video camcorder, use it for a
speech rehearsal. During video playback, pay close
attention to your facial expressions, visual directness,
posture, overall body movement, and gestures.

(Comment. See the additional exercises below for a
suggestion for videotaping speeches as they are delivered in
class.)

Additional Exercises

1. Have each student purchase a cassette for use on a
regular cassette recorder (not video). Tape a round of
speeches using the student cassettes. Give the cassettes to
the students to hear and critique on their own time. Ask
the students to pay close attention to the vocal quality,
and to articulation and pronunciation. Ask them to compare
their findings with the instructor's written criticisms for
that speech.

2. Videotape one or more rounds of student speeches.
Arrange for each student to view and critique his or her
speech or speeches, using either school playback facilities,
or the student's own equipment. Give each student a blank
critique form (such as Form A in Part II of this manual) to
use in analyzing the playback, or ask them to use a
photocopy of the form in Appendix I of the text (Figure
I.1).

Resources

Beauchene, Kathleen. "Using Quotations as Impromptu Speech
    Topics." Speech Communication Teacher 3 (Fall 1988):
    10.

Beebe, Steven A. "Eye Contact: A Nonverbal Determinant of
    Speaker Credibility." The Speech Teacher 23 (January
    1974): 21-25.

Bradley, Bert. Speech Performance. Dubuque, Iowa: Wm. C.
    Brown, 1967. The entire book concerns delivery.

Burgoon, Judee K., Buller, David B., and Woodall, W. Gill.
    Nonverbal Communication: The Unspoken Dialogue. New
    York: Harper & Row, 1989.

Glenn, Ethel C., Glenn, Phillip J., and Forman, Sandra H.
    Your Voice and Articulation, 2nd ed. Englewood Cliffs,
    N.J.: Prentice Hall, 1989.

Hahner, Jeffrey C., Sokoloff, Martin A., Salisch, Sandra, and Needler, Geoffrey D. <u>Speaking Clearly: Improving Voice and Diction</u>, 2nd ed. New York: Random House, 1986.

Harte, Thomas B., Keefe, Carolyn, and Derryberry, Bob R. <u>The Complete Book of Speechwriting for Students and Professionals</u>, 2nd ed. Edina, Minn.: Bellwether Press, 1988. Emphasizes the manuscript speech.

Leathers, Dale G. <u>Successful Nonverbal Communication: Principles and Applications</u>. New York: Macmillan, 1986.

Malandro, Loretta A., Barker, Larry L., and Barker, Deborah A. <u>Nonverbal Communication</u>, 2nd ed. New York: Random House, 1989.

Mayer, Lyle V. <u>Fundamentals of Voice and Diction</u>, 8th ed. Dubuque, Iowa: Wm. C. Brown, 1988.

Mehrabian, Albert. <u>Silent Messages</u>. Belmont, Calif.: Wadsworth, 1971. See especially Chapter 7.

Rollman, Steven A. "Classroom Exercises for Teaching Nonverbal Communication." <u>Speech Communication Teacher</u> 2 (Spring 1988): 13.

Tarver, Jerry. <u>Professional Speech Writing</u>. Richmond: Effective Speech Writing Institute, 1982. See Chapter 8 on manuscript delivery.

Wall, Jeanette. "Me? Give an Impromptu Speech? No Way!" <u>Speech Communication Teacher</u> 3 (Fall 1988): 11, 15.

Videos. "Communication by Voice and Action," 14 minutes; and "Presentation Excellence," 77 minutes. Coronet/MTI Film and Video.
The first video on voice and action focuses on the nonverbal aspects of communication. The second video, hosted by Walter Cronkite, covers a variety of presentation skills which are illustrated by film segments from the speaking of such persons as Martin Luther King, Barbara Jordan, and John F. Kennedy.

Sound filmstrip. "Impromptu Speaking," 15 minute filmstrip.
Illustrates a variety of situations that call for impromptu speaking, and provides practical suggestions for speaking effectively on the spur of the moment.

Examination Questions

Multiple-Choice

1. What type presentation is used for a speech delivered
    on the spur of the moment with no prior preparation:
    a. extemporaneous
    b. impromptu
    c. memorized
    d. entertaining
    e. informative

2. The problems of nasality, breathiness, or harshness are
    problems of what element of voice:
    a. rate
    b. pitch
    c. quality
    d. volume
    e. articulation

3. A speech that is prepared and delivered from notes (but
    is not read word for word or memorized) employs what
    type presentation:
    a. extemporaneous
    b. impromptu
    c. entertaining
    d. expository
    e. convincing

4. Chapter 13 recommends which of the following for
    speaking with a microphone:
    a. keep your mouth 1 to 2 inches from the mike
    b. ignore the mike and move around freely
    c. do not gesture or move around
    d. use memorized delivery only
    e. stand back 12 to 15 inches from the mike

5. In words per minute, what is the normal rate of
    speaking:
    a. 50 to 100
    b. 75 to 125
    c. 125 to 175
    d. 25 to 75
    e. 200 to 250

6. The distinctness or indistinctness of the individual
    sounds of human speech is called:
    a. quality
    b. pitch
    c. elocutio
    d. pronunciation
    e. articulation

7. Standards of acceptable pronunciation are based on:
    a. research by the National Bureau of Standards
    b. current usage by the leaders of society
    c. majority usage in a society
    d. the National Council of Teachers of English
    e. compilers of current dictionaries

8. According to research, what part of your physical presence receives the primary attention of the members of the audience:
    a. the face as a whole
    b. the hands
    c. the mouth
    d. the eyes
    e. your gestures

9. Which of the following is recommended by Chapter 13 for speech rehearsals:
    a. practice delivery several times while standing
    b. practice only once to avoid nervousness
    c. to make delivery fresh, do not rehearse
    d. rehearse memorized speeches only
    e. rehearse manuscript speeches only

10. Which of the following is not an element of voice:
    a. enunciation
    b. quality
    c. loudness
    d. rate
    e. pitch

Short Answer

11. Define "impromptu speaking" (one or two sentences will do).

12. Define "extemporaneous speaking" (one or two sentences will do).

13. There are six elements to the physical aspects of delivery, two being "appearance" and "facial expression." What are the other four?

    _____, _____,

    _____, and _____.

14. Indistinct and distorted speech sounds, such as saying "ress" for "rest," or "thilly" for "silly," are problems of what vocal aspect of speaking?

Discussion and Essay

15. Name and explain each of the four types of speech presentation. Discuss the advantages and disadvantages of each.

16. Name and explain each of the four elements of the speaking voice.

17. Explain the difference between "articulation" and "pronunciation." Give some examples of each.

18. Summarize the principles of preparing and using a key word note card in extemporaneous speaking.

19. Write a short essay on "Effective Bodily Communication in Public Speaking." Your answer should reveal a thorough knowledge of the content of Chapter 13.

Chapter 14

Speaking to Inform

Chapter Goals

The content of Chapter 14 should help the student achieve the following goals:

1. To understand the importance of informative speaking in a free society.

2. To understand the fundamental differences between a speech to inform and one to persuade.

3. To know the types of subjects that are suitable for speeches to inform.

4. To know the objectives of informative speaking, together with specific techniques for achieving those objectives.

Exercises from the Text

1. Think for a moment about the best teacher you have had, either in high school or in college. Make a list of the most effective teaching techniques used by this teacher. In particular, account for how the teacher motivated learning, made the material clear, and helped students remember what was covered. Make an effort to apply the items on your list to your own speaking.

(Comment. This exercise can form the basis of a class discussion. Without naming names, let the students describe some of the most effective and some of the most ineffective teachers they have known, emphasizing specific techniques of motivation, clarity, and retention.)

2. Over the next several days, listen carefully to each of your instructors as they lecture on the subject matter of the course. Do any of them begin with a statement of purpose? How many give you a preview of the main points to be covered? Can you follow the main points easily? Does the instructor conclude with a clear summary? Make a note of those teaching techniques that you find helpful, and try to apply them to your own communication. Likewise, note those things that distract or confuse you, and try to avoid them when you speak.

(Comment. This exercise can be adapted to a brief written assignment. Over a period of several days, have each student write down two or three specific techniques used by

one or more of their instructors to <u>motivate</u> learning, make
a subject <u>clear</u>, and help students <u>remember</u> what was
covered.)

Additional Exercises

1. For a round of informative speeches, have students
write in the margin of their sentence outlines the specific
places in the speech where they (a) motivate learning, (b)
make a topic clear and easy to understand, and (c) help
listeners retain information. The comments should be based
on the specific recommendations of Chapter 14 for achieving
the objectives of informative speaking.

2. Assign one of the student informative speeches in
either Appendix II or Appendix III of the text. Have
students make a photocopy of the speech, then go through
this copy marking specific techniques for achieving the
objectives of the speech, namely, motivation, clarification,
and retention. Discuss the project in class before the
papers are submitted for grading.

Resources

Baird, John E., Jr. "The Effects of Speech Summaries Upon
    Audience Comprehension of Expository Speeches of
    Varying Quality and Complexity." <u>Central States Speech
    Journal</u> 25 (Summer 1974): 119-127.

Feliciano, Gloria, Powers, Richard, and Kearl, Bryant. "The
    Presentation of Statistical Information." <u>AV
    Communication Review</u> 11 (May-June 1963): 32-39.

Frandsen, Kenneth D., and Clement, Donald A. "The Functions
    of Human Communication in Informing: Communicating and
    Processing Information." In Carroll C. Arnold and John
    Waite Bowers, eds., <u>Handbook of Rhetorical and
    Communication Theory</u>. Boston: Allyn and Bacon.

Fregoe, David H. "Informative vs. Persuasive Speaking: The
    Objects Game." <u>Speech Communication Teacher</u> 3 (Winter
    1989): 13-14.

Klein, Stephen B. <u>Learning: Principles and Applications</u>.
    New York: McGraw-Hill, 1987.

Olbricht, Thomas H. <u>Informative Speaking</u>. Glenview, Ill.:
    Scott, Foresman, 1968.

Rowan, Katherine. "The Speech to Explain Difficult Ideas."
    <u>Speech Communication Teacher</u> 4 (Summer 1990): 2-3.

111

Shamo, G. Wayne, and Bittner, John R. "Recall as a Function
    of Language Style." <u>Southern Speech Communication
    Journal</u> 38 (Winter 1972): 181-187.

Spicer, Christopher, and Bassett, Ronald E. "The Effect of
    Organization on Learning from an Informative Message."
    <u>Southern Speech Communication Journal</u> 41 (Spring
    1976): 290-299.

Walter, Otis M. <u>Speaking to Inform and Persuade</u>, 2nd ed.
    New York: Macmillan, 1982. See especially Chapters 2,
    3, and 4 on the informative speech.

**Video. "Reporting and Briefing," 16 minute video.
    Coronet/MTI Film and Video.**
    Focuses on preparing and delivering oral reports, with
    recommendations for being clear, accurate, and
    interesting.

**Sound filmstrips. "Types of Information," and "Structure
    and Rehearsal," each filmstrip 15 minutes in length.
    Films for the Humanities.**
    This filmstrip set presents the preparation and
    delivery of informative speeches. Includes attention
    to audience analysis for informative speaking, as well
    as various ways to support points with materials that
    help achieve clarity and maintain interest.

Examination Questions

<u>Multiple-Choice</u>

1. The basic goal of an informative speech is to:
    a. keep audience alert and interested
    b. use knowledge to change audience attitudes
    c. get listeners to act wisely
    d. achieve understanding
    e. create good will

2. A speech on "The Rules for Playing Soccer" illustrates
    what type of subject for a speech to inform:
    a. speech about events
    b. speech about processes and procedures
    c. speech about people
    d. speech about definitions and concepts
    e. speech about tangible objects

3. One way to motivate your audience to learn from an informative speech is to:
   a. always preview the main points
   b. employ oral signposts as you speak
   c. use both positive and negative incentives
   d. use humor extensively
   e. use concrete language

4. Which of the following is not a technique for achieving clarity in an informative speech:
   a. state the central idea clearly
   b. summarize the main points
   c. use visual aids
   d. use positive incentives
   e. explain the unfamiliar with the familiar

5. An instructor who says "learn this material or you will flunk the exam," is using what technique related to informative speaking:
   a. curiosity
   b. negative incentive
   c. ethos
   d. pathos
   e. positive incentive

6. According to research, visual aids are effective, and often essential, in helping an audience understand:
   a. great battles
   b. how to make something
   c. how to clean a VCR
   d. what machinery does
   e. statistics

7. Chapter 14 says that establishing credibility with the audience helps with what objective of informative speaking:
   a. motivation
   b. clarification
   c. sustaining attention and interest
   d. retention of knowledge
   e. motivating decision and action

8. Chapter 14 describes two specific types of positive incentive, one of which is "reward"; what is the second?
   a. the enjoyment of humor
   b. satisfy curiosity
   c. satisfaction of having knowledge
   d. establishing one's ethos
   e. to be accepted by the group

9. In addition to <u>motivation</u> and <u>clarification</u>, which of
    these is a key objective of informative speaking:
    a. entertaining
    b. changing negative attitudes
    c. retention of information
    d. to get listeners to take good notes
    e. stay within the time limit

10. A speech on Washington's design of Mount Vernon
    illustrates what type of subject for informative
    speaking:
    a. speech about people
    b. speech about objects and areas
    c. speech about events
    d. speech about definitions
    e. speech about processes and procedures

Short Answer

11. In informing, you should explain the unfamiliar in
    terms of:

    _____.

12. What are the three key objectives of informative
    speaking?

    _____, _____,

    and _____.

13. As explained in Chapter 14, what is the basic goal of
    informative speaking?

Discussion and Essay

14. Explain, compare, and contrast the goal of informative
    speaking with the goal of persuasive speaking.

15. Discuss the place of informative speaking in a
    democratic society. Give specific examples.

16. Name and explain each of the three objectives of
    informative speaking. Include specific recommendations
    for how each objective can be achieved.

Chapter 15

The Means of Persuasion

Chapter Goals

The content of Chapter 15 should help the student achieve the following goals:

1.   To better understand what is meant by persuasion, including the importance of the audience, the specific purpose, and rhetorical proof to persuasive speaking.

2.   To understand the three primary means of persuasion, namely, logos, ethos, and pathos.

3.   To know the reasoning processes of induction, deduction, causal relation, and parallel case, including how to employ them in persuasive speaking.

4.   To better understand ethos and how to establish it in the context of persuasive speaking.

5.   To better understand pathos, including appeals to human emotions, needs, and values, and to learn how to employ pathos in a persuasive speech.

Exercises from the Text

1.   While listening to speeches in various campus and community settings, make notes on those characteristics of speakers that help establish credibility, as well as those that diminish credibility. Compare your findings with the discussion of ethos in this chapter, then apply your conclusions to your own speaking. What specific things should you do to better achieve strong credibility with your audiences?

(Comment. Assign this exercise for a brief written report. Each student should attend a speaking event, taking notes on the persuasiveness of both prior ethos and demonstrated ethos. Tell the students to be specific, such as noting ways in which prior ethos was established, and how the speaker's content, use of language, and delivery affected ethos during the speech. On the day the assignment is due, lead the class in a discussion of the findings. Include attention to those things that lowered speaker credibility.)

2.   Study Martin Luther King's "I Have a Dream" speech (the text is in Appendix III), paying particular attention to King's use of pathos. Using the discussion of pathos in this chapter as a guide, write down as many appeals to

specific emotions, needs, and values as you can identify in
this famous speech.

(Comment. This exercise can form the basis for a class
analysis and discussion of pathos. Have each student make a
photocopy of King's speech, marking his appeals to specific
emotions, needs, and values in the margins of the page. The
project can be submitted for grading after the class has
discussed the various psychological appeals that are
identified.)

Additional Exercises

1.   Make copies of the student speech from Part IV of this
manual and distribute to the class. Ask the students to
study the logos of the speech, writing in the margin the
types of evidence and reasoning used by the speaker.

2.   Ask each student to construct four persuasive arguments
(one inductive, one deductive, one causal, and one by
parallel case). The arguments should be written out in full
in language suitable for a public speech. Remind the
students to apply the tests for the various forms of
reasoning to their examples before turning in the paper. If
time permits, have each student read an example or two in
class for analysis and discussion by the group.

3.   For the next round of persuasive speeches, have each
student submit two copies of the speech outline. One copy
should be done as usual; the second copy should have notes
in the margins about specific uses of forms of reasoning,
credibility appeals, and appeals to emotions, needs, and
values. At a minimum, each student should identify at least
one logical argument, one way in which credibility is
established, and one psychological appeal in the outline.
If the class does a manuscript speech, this project can be
applied to the manuscript rather than to the outline.

Resources

Benoit, William L. "Argument and Credibility Appeals in
     Persuasion." Southern Speech Communication Journal 52
     (Winter 1987): 181-197.

Bostrom, Robert N., and Tucker, Raymond K. "Evidence,
     Personality, and Attitude Change." Speech Monographs
     36 (March 1969): 22-27.

Campbell, Karlyn K. The Rhetorical Act. Belmont, Calif.:
     Wadsworth, 1981. See especially Chapter 6 on ethos.

Huber, Robert B. Influencing Through Argument. New York:
    David McKay, 1963.

Kahane, Howard. Logic and Contemporary Rhetoric: The Use
    of Reason in Everyday Life, 5th ed. Belmont, Calif.:
    Wadsworth, 1988.

Larson, Charles U. Persuasion: Reception and
    Responsibility, 5th ed. Belmont, Calif.: Wadsworth,
    1989.

Maslow, A. H. Motivation and Personality, 2nd ed. New
    York: Harper & Row, 1970.

McCroskey, James C. "A Summary of Experimental Research on
    the Effects of Evidence in Persuasive Communication."
    Quarterly Journal of Speech 55 (April 1969): 169-176.

McCroskey, James C., and Young, Thomas J. "Ethos and
    Credibility: The Construct and Its Measurement After
    Three Decades." Central States Speech Journal 32
    (Spring 1981): 24-34.

O'Keefe, Daniel J. Persuasion: Theory and Research.
    Newbury Park, Calif.: Sage Publications, 1990.

Rokeach, Milton. The Nature of Human Values. New York:
    The Free Press, 1973.

Ross, Raymond S. Understanding Persuasion: Foundations and
    Practice, 2nd ed. Englewood Cliffs, N.J.:
    Prentice-Hall, 1985.

Simons, Herbert W. Persuasion: Understanding, Practice,
    and Analysis. New York: Random House, 1986.

Sound filmstrips. "Understanding Persuasion," and
    "Reason and Emotion," each filmstrip 15 minutes
    in length. Films for the Humanities.
    These filmstrips discuss logical proof, speaker
    credibility, and the use of emotional appeals in
    persuasive speaking.

Examination Questions

<u>Multiple-Choice</u>

1.   Reasoning from specific instances to a general
      conclusion about those instances is called:
      a.   parallel case
      b.   using a syllogism
      c.   induction
      d.   deduction
      e.   argument from analogy

2.   Aristotle said that speaker credibility involved 3
      elements: knowledge, good will, and what third
      element?
      a.   friendliness
      b.   sincerity
      c.   pathos
      d.   mastery of induction and deduction
      e.   good character

3.   If you employ fear, pity, or sympathy in a speech, what
      type of proof are you using?
      a.   appeal to needs
      b.   appeal to emotions
      c.   appeal to values
      d.   figurative analogy appeals
      e.   cause-to-effect appeals

4.   When we reason from the general to the specific, saying
      that what is true of a class of things applies to a
      member of that class, what type reasoning are we using?
      a.   inductive
      b.   deductive
      c.   parallel case
      d.   effect-to-cause
      e.   cause-to-effect

5.   The proof that emerges from the set of attitudes that
      the audience holds about the speaker is called:
      a.   pathos
      b.   logos
      c.   ethos
      d.   inventio
      e.   elocutio

6.   An argument stated according to a major premise, a
      minor premise, and a conclusion, is called:
      a.   a syllogism
      b.   an induction
      c.   reasoning from cause to effect
      d.   reasoning by parallel case
      e.   reasoning from the specific to the general

7. A speaker who argues that a scholarship program for
    debate would work well in your college because a
    similar program has worked well in another college is
    using what form of reasoning:
    a. a syllogism
    b. induction
    c. cause to effect
    d. effect to cause
    e. parallel case

8. The reputation that precedes a speaker (what the
    audience knows in advance) is called:
    a. a priori evidence
    b. demonstrated ethos
    c. prior ethos
    d. disposito
    e. causal reasoning

9. The <u>first</u> level of human need in Maslow's heirarchy of
    needs is:
    a. safety
    b. security
    c. self-esteem
    d. physiological
    e. to be loved and accepted by others

10. Psychologist Milton Rokeach is a leading authority on:
    a. rational persuasion
    b. human values
    c. cognitive dissonance
    d. fallacy in human thinking
    e. subliminal persuasion

Short Answer

11. Complete this definition: "Persuasive speaking is
    spoken discourse that . . . "

    _____.

12. Your supporting evidence in a persuasive speech should
    meet what three standards?

    _____, _____,

    and _____.

13. What are the two tests of induction?

14. What are the two tests of deduction?

15. What are the two tests of reasoning by parallel case?

16. Name two of the three tests for causal reasoning.

17. Give two examples of positive emotions, and two examples of negative emotions:

    positive:_____ and _____.

    negative:_____ and _____.

Discussion and Essay

18. Explain logical proof (logos) as a means of persuasion.

19. Explain speaker credibility (ethos) as a means of persuasion.

20. Explain psychological appeals (pathos) as a means of persuasion.

21. What is meant by "qualifying your source" in persuasive speaking? Discuss and give a good example or two.

22. Explain Maslow's heirarchy of needs and how the concept can be useful to the persuasive speaker.

23. Explain Rokeach's value theory, including instrumental and terminal values. Give some examples. How is value theory of use to the persuasive speaker?

Chapter 16

Speaking to Persuade

Chapter Goals

The content of Chapter 16 should help the student achieve the following goals:

1. To know the three types of persuasive speeches as classified by audience attitude toward the speaker's specific purpose.

2. To understand when to emphasize logical proof, when to emphasize psychological proof, and when to employ a balance in logical and psychological proof in persuasive speaking.

3. To understand the logical argument and argument/counter-argument approaches to persuasive speaking.

4. To understand the cognitive consistency approach to persuasive speaking.

5. To understand the reward/penalty approach to persuasive speaking.

Exercises from the Text

1. Before your next persuasive speech in your public speaking course, conduct a poll of the attitudes of your classmates on the topic of your speech (you will find suggestions for doing this in Chapters 5). Use the results of your poll to determine your general persuasive purpose, that is, whether your speech is to convince, to actuate, or to reinforce.

(Comment. The instructor could require each student to poll the class regarding attitudes on a subject for a persuasive speech. The students should be advised to phrase their questions carefully in order to get dependable results. See the suggestions in Chapter 5.)

2. After studying the cognitive consistency approach to persuasion as explained in this chapter, make a list of student attitudes and/or actions that you believe are inconsistent with each other (this attitude and that attitude or behavior don't go together). Use the list to plan a speech to your class (or other student group) based on the cognitive consistency approach to persuasion.

(<u>Comment</u>. This exercise could form the basis for a round of
persuasive speeches by requiring that the speeches be based
on the cognitive consistency approach. An alternative is to
ask each student to prepare a list of at least three good
topics for classroom speeches that include arguments based
on cognitive consistency theory. The list could be
submitted for grading.)

Additional Exercises

1.   Have students turn in a list of specific purposes for
persuasive speeches that are suitable for delivery to the
public speaking class. The list should include at least
three to convince, three to actuate, and three to reinforce.
If this is done early in the unit on persuasion, it can
provide the students with ideas for classroom speeches.

2.   The section on "Exercises from the Text" above asks for
a speech based on the cognitive consistency approach to
persuasion. The instructor can assign one of the other
research-based approaches as an alternative speaking
project, that is: a speech based on the logical argument
approach; a speech based on the argument/counter-argument
approach; or a speech based on the reward/penalty approach.
An alternative is to give students a choice by assigning a
persuasive speech, specifying that it must be based on one
of the four research-based approaches. Be sure to ask the
students to label the approach they have used.

Resources

(Note: In addition to the resources listed below, review
those given above for Chapter 15, "The Means of Persuasion."
The **sound filmstrips** on persuasion listed for Chapter 15 are
suitable for use in connection with either Chapter 15 or
Chapter 16).

Anderson, Loren J. "A Summary of Research on Order Effects
     in Communication." In Jimmie D. Trent, Judith S.
     Trent, and Daniel J. O'Neill, eds., <u>Concepts in
     Communication</u>. Boston: Allyn and Bacon, 1973.

Bettinghaus, Erwin, and Cody, Michael. <u>Persuasive
     Communication</u>, 4th ed. New York: Holt, Rinehart and
     Winston, 1987. See pp. 153-160 for a review of the
     literature on reward and penalty in persuasion.

Burgoon, Michael, and Burgoon, Judee K.   "Message Strategies
     in Influence Attempts." In G. J. Hanneman and W. J.
     McEwen, eds., <u>Communication and Behavior</u>. Reading,
     Mass.: Addison-Wesley, 1975.

Dickens, Milton. Speech: Dynamic Communication, 3rd ed.
New York: Harcourt Brace Jovanovich, 1974. See
especially Chapters 14, 15, and 16 for discussions of
speeches to reinforce, to convince, and to actuate.

Festinger, Leon. A Theory of Cognitive Dissonance.
Stanford: Stanford University Press, 1957.

O'Keefe, Daniel J. Persuasion: Theory and Research.
Newbury Park, Calif.: Sage Publications, 1990. See
Chapter 4 on "Cognitive Dissonance Theory," and Chapter
5 on the "Theory of Reasoned Action."

Schreier, Howard N. "Analyzing Persuasive Tactics." Speech
Communication Teacher 3 (Summer 1989): 14.

Strong, W. F., and Cook, John A. Persuasion: A Practical
Guide to Effective Persuasive Speech. Dubuque, Iowa:
Kendall/Hunt, 1987. This text emphasizes the use of
cognitive consistency in persuasive speaking.

Verderber, Rudolph F. The Challenge of Effective Speaking,
7th ed. Belmont, Calif.: Wadsworth, 1988. Includes
chapters on the speech to convince and the speech to
actuate.

Examination Questions

Multiple-Choice

1. When your audience has a favorable attitude toward your
    subject, but is not doing anything about it, what type
    of speech should you plan:
    a. expository
    b. to convince
    c. to actuate
    d. to reinforce
    e. to inspire

2. When the audience has a strongly unfavorable attitude
    toward your topic, what type of speech should you plan:
    a. expository
    b. to convince
    c. to actuate
    d. to reinforce
    e. to stimulate

3. A speech of inspiration, such as a commencement
    address, is also called a speech to:
    a. entertain
    b. convince
    c. actuate
    d. reinforce
    e. inform

4. What type of speech did John F. Kennedy deliver to the
    Houston ministers in the campaign of 1960:
    a. to inform
    b. to entertain
    c. to convince
    d. to actuate
    e. to reinforce

5. If your audience has a favorable attitude toward your
    subject, and is supporting that attitude with action,
    what type of speech is called for:
    a. to inform
    b. to entertain
    c. to convince
    d. to actuate
    e. to reinforce

6. What type of response is sought in a convincing speech:
    a. overt response
    b. mental agreement
    c. new action
    d. a clear understanding
    e. strongly emotional

7. The speech to reinforce emphasizes what means of
    persuasion:
    a. ethos
    b. logos
    c. pathos
    d. cause to effect
    e. strong logical argument and evidence

8. An "overt response" is one that is:
    a. highly logical
    b. highly emotional
    c. in the mind
    d. observable
    e. based on emotional excess

9. Abraham Lincoln's "Gettysburg Address" is an example of
    what type of speech:
    a. to convince
    b. to actuate
    c. to reinforce
    d. to create good will
    e. campaign speech for public office

10. What approach to persuasion is appropriate for persons whose values, attitudes, and actions are not in harmony with each other:
    a. motivated sequence
    b. argument/counter-argument
    c. cognitive consistency
    d. reward/penalty
    e. expository

Short Answer

11. Chapter 16 lists three methods for getting others to do what you want. The first of these is "coercion." What are the other two?

    _____and_____.

12. An attitude is defined as:

    _____.

13. For the speech to convince, the audience attitude is:

    _____.

14. For the speech to actuate, the audience attitude is:

    _____.

15. For the speech to reinforce, the audience attitude is:

    _____.

Discussion and Essay

16. Define and explain the speech to convince, including when it is appropriate, and the primary means of persuasion that should be used.

17. Define and explain the speech to actuate, including when it is appropriate, and the primary means of persuasion that should be used.

18. Define and explain the speech to reinforce, including when it is appropriate, and the primary means of persuasion that should be used.

19. Explain the argument/counter-argument approach to persuasive speaking.

20. Explain the cognitive consistency approach to persuasive speaking.

21. Explain the reward/penalty approach to persuasive speaking.

Chapter 17

Special Forms and Occasions

Chapter Goals

The content of Chapter 17 should help the student achieve the following goals:

1. To learn how to prepare special forms of persuasive speeches, including speeches of inspiration, nomination, and good will.

2. To learn how to prepare speeches of courtesy, including speeches of introduction, welcome, presentation, and response.

3. To learn how to prepare an entertaining speech.

Exercises from the Text

1. Assume that you are to nominate a student acquaintance for class president, or for some other campus office. Interview that person, then prepare a short speech of nomination for the office you have chosen.

(Comment. This exercise could be assigned as a short manuscript speech to be turned in and graded. If a campus election is pending, the exercise can be made more realistic by having each student in the class interview an actual candidate for campus office, then writing out a nominating speech for that candidate.)

2. Select a company, organization, or cause that you like and support. Outline a speech of good will for your choice, assuming that your audience will be a local civic club (such as Rotary, or the Junior Chamber of Commerce).

(Comment. A good will speech makes an excellent assignment for a round of persuasive speeches to be delivered in class. It is especially appropriate for students who are interested in the field of public relations, for public relations work often includes preparing messages of good will on behalf of one's employer.)

3. During the next several weeks or months, listen carefully to the speeches of introduction you hear on campus and in the community. Evaluate the effectiveness of each introduction, and adapt what you learn to your own speaking.

(Comment. This exercise can be assigned for a written or oral report, having each student evaluate at least one speech of introduction during the term. The assignment should be made early in the course, to be submitted near the end of the course. On the day the project is due, lead the students in a discussion of what they do and do not like in an introduction.)

4.   Assume that you are to introduce a classmate to your speech class. After an interview, prepare a one-minute introduction that would be suitable for that person's next classroom speech.

(Comment. This exercise is similar to one described for Chapter 2. However, a short speech introducing a classmate can be incorporated into a round of speeches later in the course. For example, some instructors have students introduce one another in conjunction with the final speech of the course.)

Additional Exercises

1.   Assign a speech of inspiration for a round of classroom speeches. One choice would be a eulogy, in which the speaker would research the life of a famous person whom he or she admired, then speak in praise of that person. A second choice would be a speech of commemoration concerning an important event, the founding and achievements of an institution, or the accomplishments of a group of people.

2.   Assign a speech of entertainment for a round of classroom speeches. Remind the students that a speech to entertain should consist of something more than telling several "jokes." Rather, it should be developed around a central theme and have form and unity, even though its primary purpose is to amuse, delight, and please.

Resources

Harte, Thomas B., Keefe, Carolyn, and Derryberry, Bob R. The Complete Book of Speechwriting for Students and Professionals, 2nd ed. Edina, Minn.: Bellwether Press, 1988. See especially Chapter 14, which concerns speaking on special occasions.

King, Robert G. Forms of Public Address. Indianapolis: Bobbs-Merrill, 1969.

Lyle, Guy R., and Guinagh, Kevin., comps. I Am Happy to Present. New York: H. W. Wilson, 1953. A collection of various types of introductions.

Majors, Randall E. "Practical Ceremonial Speaking: Three
    Speech Activities." Speech Communication Teacher 3
    (Winter 1989): 2-3.

Rogge, Edward, and Ching, James C. Advanced Public
    Speaking. New York: Holt, Rinehart and Winston, 1966.
    See especially Chapter 11 on the speech to entertain.

Yeager, Willard H. Effective Speaking for Every Occasion,
    2nd ed. New York: Prentice-Hall, 1951.

**Sound filmstrip. "Special Speech Occasions," 15 minutes.
    Films for the Humanities.**
    Covers various forms of speeches, such as
    introductions, speeches of tribute and acceptance, and
    after-dinner speeches.

Examination Questions

Multiple-Choice

1. An occasion of commemoration or celebration is a time
    for what type of speech:
    a. to entertain
    b. expository
    c. to inspire
    d. good will
    e. response

2. A talk honoring the life of some deceased person is
    called:
    a. speech of good will
    b. speech to convince
    c. speech of celebration
    d. eulogy
    e. speech of response

3. A nominating speech is a persuasive speech:
    a. to convince
    b. to actuate
    c. to reinforce
    d. to inspire
    e. to achieve good will

4. The speech of commemoration concerns:
    a. past events or accomplishments
    b. recognition of current achievements
    c. welcome of guests
    d. giving an award to a worthy person
    e. an expository historical lecture

5. A public relations representative of a college who makes a speech to win friends for the school is making what type of speech:
    a. to convince
    b. to actuate
    c. to entertain
    d. good will
    e. informative

6. According to Chapter 17, which of these is not a speech of courtesy:
    a. introduction
    b. response
    c. welcome
    d. nomination
    e. presentation

7. A speech to change audience behavior that makes extensive and effective use of interesting stories and humor should be classified as a speech to:
    a. reinforce
    b. entertain
    c. convince
    d. actuate
    e. stimulate

8. The eulogy, the speech of commemoration, and the speech of celebration are all variations of what type of speech:
    a. informative
    b. inspirational
    c. entertaining
    d. presentation
    e. actuation

9. An after-dinner speech planned to delight and please the audience is an example of what type of speech:
    a. reinforcing
    b. actuating
    c. inspirational
    d. stimulating
    e. entertaining

10. What type of speech would you prepare to praise the life of some great American, such as Thomas Jefferson or Eleanor Roosevelt:
    a. expository
    b. good will
    c. eulogy
    d. convincing
    e. celebration

Short Answer

11. What special type of speech is called for in each of the following situations:

    a. A speech honoring the life of Martin Luther King, Jr.

       _____.

    b. A speech delivered by a member of the senior class at a college graduation ceremony.

       _____.

    c. A short speech announcing a school's award for "outstanding debater of the year," to be concluded with the awarding of a trophy to the winner.

       _____.

12. What are the three standards of a speech of courtesy?

    a._____.

    b._____.

    c._____.

Discussion and Essay

13. Define a eulogy and explain how to prepare one.

14. Define the speech of good will, and discuss how to prepare one.

15. Explain the preparation of a speech of introduction (introducing another person to the audience).

16. Define the speech to entertain, and discuss how to prepare one.

Appendix I

Speech Criticism: Analyzing and
Evaluating Public Speeches

Goals of Appendix

The essay on speech criticism should help the student
achieve the following goals:

1.   To learn what is meant by "speech criticism."

2.   To understand the important functions of speech
      criticism in a democratic society.

3.   To learn how to do speech criticism, including speech
      analysis and speech evaluation.

Exercises from the Text

1.   Make a photocopy of the Public Speaking Comments Form.
Attend a campus or community event that features a public
speaker, filling out the form as you listen. If the speaker
were to ask you for a brief critique, what specific
recommendations would you make for improving content and
delivery?

(Comment. This exercise can be done by making copies of the
form as printed on pp. 342-343 of the text, or the
instructor can make copies of the onepage version given
below. Both have the same items for analysis and
evaluation, and the same threepoint scoring system.)

2.   Choose one of the student speeches from Appendix II or
Appendix III for analysis and evaluation. Focus your
criticism on the elements of organization, reasoning, and
evidence. List specific strong and weak points for each of
these elements. As a result of this exercise, what ideas do
you get for improving the organization, reasoning, and
evidence of your own speeches?

(Comment. An alternative is for the instructor to make
copies of the student speech from Part IV of this manual.
Have the students analyze and evaluate the speech, writing
their comments in the margin provided for this purpose.)

3.   When you are listening to a speech, you usually give at
least some attention to a variety of rhetorical elements (as
illustrated by items 1 through 10 of the comments form).
However, you can do speech criticism that is limited to just
one rhetorical element, such as speech organization, the use
of evidence, or how well the speaker analyzed the audience.

Here are some suggestions for speech criticism focused on one element.

    a.   Criticize the delivery of a campus speech. Be thorough, covering general physical appearance, visual directness, bodily movement and gesture, and voice, articulation, and pronunciation. For ideas, see Chapter 13 of this text.

    b.   Criticize the language of a great speech from American history (such as one of those in Appendix III). Include the standards of clarity, appropriateness, and vividness. For other ideas on language, see Chapter 12 of this text.

    c.   From a campus or community speech, criticize one of the following rhetorical elements: use of logical reasoning; holding audience interest; achieving clarity; effectiveness of introduction and conclusion; building speaker ethos; ethics and social consequences.

(Comment. For any of the projects mentioned in this exercise, the instructor can provide the students with a copy of the critique form used by the instructor to evaluate classroom speeches, or a copy of the onepage analysis and evaluation form that matches the one on pp. 342-343 of the text.)

Additional Exercises

1.   Give each student a copy of John F. Kennedy's speech to the Houston ministers as provided in Part IV of this manual (or a copy of some other speech favored by the instructor). Have the students analyze and evaluate the arguments, evidence (various types and quality of supporting materials), and language of the speech. Space is provided in the left-hand margin for students to record specific comments. For a major project in speech criticism, assign a "critical essay" concerning Kennedy's Houston speech.

2.   In addition to the Public Speaking Comments Form provided below, there is a second, simplified form covering content and delivery in a broad way (with space for other items that students might wish to note). This simplified Student Comments Form can be duplicated and used for student criticism of speeches delivered in class. Be sure to assign Appendix I in connection with these in-class criticisms.

Resources

Andrews, James R. The Practice of Rhetorical Criticism, 2nd
    ed. White Plains, N.Y.: Longman, 1990.

Arnold, Carroll C. The Criticism of Oral Rhetoric.
    Columbus, Ohio: Charles E. Merrill, 1974.

Bitzer, Lloyd F. "The Rhetorical Situation." Philosophy
    and Rhetoric 1 (Winter 1968): 1-14.

Cathcart, Robert. Post Communication: Rhetorical Analysis
    and Evaluation, 2nd ed. Indianapolis: Bobbs-Merrill,
    1981.

Downey, Sharon, and Rasmussen, Karen. "A Claim-Making
    Exercise for Critical Writing in Rhetoric." Speech
    Communication Teacher 4 (Spring 1990): 10-11.

"Focus On Teaching Rhetorical Criticism." Special issue of
    Communication Education 38 (July 1989): 175-213.
    This symposium concerning undergraduate speech
    criticism consists of six articles: "Teaching
    Rhetorical Criticism to Undergraduates," by Martin J.
    Medhurst; "'Wise Skepticism': On the Education of a
    Young Critic," by James R. Andrews; "Rhetorical
    Criticism in the Liberal Arts Curriculum," by Bruce E.
    Gronbeck; "Rhetorical Criticism as the Asking of
    Questions," by Sonja K. Foss; "Thematic Approaches to
    Teaching Rhetoric Criticism," by David Henry and Harry
    Sharp, Jr.,; and "Rhetorical Criticism: Forensic
    Communication in the Written Mode," by Martin J.
    Medhurst. Highly recommended to the instructor who
    teaches speech criticism as a part of the public
    speaking course.

Foss, Sonja K. Rhetorical Criticism: Exploration and
    Practice. Prospect Heights, Ill.: Waveland Press,
    1989.

Hart, Roderick P. Modern Rhetorical Criticism. Glenview,
    Ill.: Scott, Foresman/Little, Brown Higher Education,
    1990.

Jensen, Marvin D. "The Gettysburg Address: Exploring
    Lincoln's Second Thoughts." Speech Communication
    Teacher 4 (Summer 1990): 10.

Thonssen, Lester, Baird, A. Craig, and Braden, Waldo W.
    Speech Criticism, 2nd ed. New York: Ronald Press,
    1970.

Video (speeches). Multi-volume set of speeches on
    videotape. The Educational Video Group.
    Excellent source of videos of speeches for student
    analysis and evaluation. Includes videos of complete
    speeches by persons such as Franklin Roosevelt, Winston
    Churchill, Douglas MacArthur, Adlai Stevenson, Dwight

Eisenhower, Martin Luther King, Jr., Jesse Jackson, Barbara Jordan, Hubert Humphrey, Mario Cuomo, and Ronald Reagan.

Examination Questions

(Note: the content of the essay on speech criticism does not lend itself well to multiple-choice questions. Therefore, only short answer and discussion/essay questions are given below.)

Short Answer

1.   Appendix I defines speech criticism as:_____

    _____ .

2.   Speech <u>evaluation</u> should assess what three things?

    a._____ .

    b._____ .

    c._____ .

3.   How does Lloyd Bitzer define an "exigence" in his essay on "The Rhetorical Situation"?

4.   In addition to addressing human problems, what is a second reason for a speech to be made?

Discussion and Essay

5.   Explain what is covered by the topic "speech analysis."

6.   What would you cover in evaluating the "effectiveness" of a speech? Discuss.

7.   What would you cover in evaluating the "artistic quality" of a speech? Discuss.

8.   What would you cover in evaluating the "social worth" of a speech? Discuss.

PUBLIC SPEAKING COMMENTS FORM

Speaker: _____ Topic: _____

Encircle 1 for <u>below average</u>, 2 for <u>average</u>, and 3 for <u>above average</u>.

<u>THE SPEECH: Comments</u>

1. **CHOICE OF SUBJECT**   1 2 3
    Appropriate to speaker,
    audience, & occasion

2. **INTRODUCTION**   1 2 3
    Gain attention
    Orient to topic
    Clear central idea

3. **BODY**   1 2 3
    Main points, content
    Sound reasoning & evidence
    Holds interest

4. **CONCLUSION**   1 2 3
    Summary, clarity
    Persuasiveness
    Originality

<u>SPEECH PRESENTATION: Comments</u>

5. **LANGUAGE**   1 2 3
    Appropriate, clear,
    vivid

6. **VOICE AND DICTION**   1 2 3
    Vocal variety
    Distinct articulation
    Standard pronunciation

7. **BODILY COMMUNICATION**   1 2 3
    Visual directness, posture,
    movement, & gesture

<u>THE SPEAKER (ethos): Comments</u>

8. **SPEAKER CREDIBILITY**   1 2 3
    Good will
    Good character
    Expertise

<u>AUDIENCE ANALYSIS: Comments</u>

9. **ANALYSIS OF AUDIENCE BY SPEAKER**   1 2 3
    Attitudes
    Knowledge
    Interests

<u>OVERALL EVALUATION: Comments</u>

10. **EFFECTIVENESS, SOCIAL CONSEQUENCES**   1 2 3
    Clarity, persuasiveness
    Holding interest
    Ethics & social consequences

<u>OTHER COMMENTS</u>. In the space below, note what you like best about the speech, as well as your major recommendations for improvement. Use back of sheet if necessary.

PUBLIC SPEAKING: STUDENT COMMENTS FORM

Speaker:_____Date:_____

Topic:_____

Student Evaluator:_____

Write in your comments about the strong points of the speech, as well as your suggestions for improvement.

SPEECH CONTENT: choice of subject; introduction, body, and conclusion; main points and support.

SPEECH PRESENTATION: language, voice, articulation, pronunciation; visual directness, movement, and gesture.

OVERALL EVALUATION: clarity; persuasiveness; holding interest; social consequences; effectiveness.

Overall, I rate this speech:
   ( )   1 (below average; needs improvement)
   ( )   2 (average; good, but can be better)
   ( )   3 (above average; well done)

OTHER COMMENTS:
What did you like best about this speech?

What are your major recommendations for improvement?

PART IV

ADDITIONAL SPEECHES FOR STUDY
AND DISCUSSION

Here are two additional speeches to supplement those provided in Appendix II and Appendix III of the text. The first is the complete text of John F. Kennedy's speech on separation of church and state, delivered to the Greater Houston Ministerial Association during the presidential campaign of 1960. This speech is discussed on pp. 302-303 of Public Speaking in a Free Society as an example of an effective speech to convince. The text provided here is from a tape recording of the speech.

The second is a student persuasive speech delivered in the competition of the Interstate Oratorical Association, and published in Winning Orations, 1989. It is reprinted here with the permission of the Interstate Oratorical Association. A "comments" space is provided in the left margin of each page to facilitate use of the transcripts for assignments in speech criticism.

SPEECH TO THE GREATER HOUSTON MINISTERIAL ASSOCIATION

by John F. Kennedy

PRESCRIPTIONS FOR AN OLD PROBLEM

by Kimberly Fisher

SPEECH TO THE GREATER HOUSTON
MINISTERIAL ASSOCIATION

John F. Kennedy

(John F. Kennedy delivered this speech to the Greater
Houston Ministerial Association on September 12, 1960,
during the presidential campaign of that year.)

----

1   I am grateful for your generous
invitation to state my views.

2   While the so-called religious issue is
necessarily and properly the chief topic here
tonight, I want to emphasize from the outset
that I believe that we have far more critical
issues in the 1960 election: the spread of
Communist influence, until it now festers
only ninety miles off the coast of
Florida--the humiliating treatment of our
President and Vice President by those who no
longer respect our power--the hungry children
I saw in West Virginia, the old people who
cannot pay their doctor's bills, the families
forced to give up their farms--an America
with too many slums, with too few schools,
and too late to the moon and outer space.

3   These are the real issues which should
decide this campaign. And they are not
religious issues--for war and hunger and
ignorance and despair know no religious
barrier.

4   But because I am a Catholic, and no
Catholic has ever been elected President, the
real issues in this campaign have been
obscured--perhaps deliberately, in some
quarters less responsible than this. So it
is apparently necessary for me to state once
again--not what kind of church I believe in,
for that should be important only to me, but
what kind of America I believe in.

5   I believe in an America where the
separation of church and state is
absolute--where no Catholic prelate would
tell the President (should he be a Catholic)
how to act and no Protestant minister would
tell his parishioners for whom to vote--where
no church or church school is granted any

public funds or political preference--and
where no man is denied public office merely
because his religion differs from the
President who might appoint him or the people
who might elect him.

6   I believe in an America that is
officially neither Catholic, Protestant nor
Jewish--where no public official either
requests or accepts instructions on public
policy from the Pope, the National Council of
Churches or any other ecclesiastical
source--where no religious body seeks to
impose its will directly or indirectly upon
the general populace or the public acts of
its officials--and where religious liberty is
so indivisible that an act against one church
is treated as an act against all.

7   For, while this year it may be a
Catholic against whom the finger of suspicion
is pointed, in other years it has been, and
may someday be again, a Jew--or a Quaker--or
a Unitarian--or a Baptist. It was Virginia's
harassment of Baptist preachers, for example,
that led to Jefferson's statute of religious
freedom. Today, I may be the victim--but
tomorrow it may be you--until the whole
fabric of our harmonious society is ripped
apart at a time of great national peril.

8   Finally, I believe in an America where
religious intolerance will someday end--where
all men and all churches are treated as
equal--where every man has the same right to
attend or not to attend the church of his
choice--where there is no Catholic vote, no
anti-Catholic vote, no bloc voting of any
kind--and where Catholics, Protestants and
Jews, both the lay and the pastoral level,
will refrain from those attitudes of disdain
and division which have so often marred their
works in the past, and promote instead the
American ideal of brotherhood.

9   That is the kind of America in which I
believe. And it represents the kind of
Presidency in which I believe--a great office
that must be neither humbled by making it the
instrument of any religious group, nor
tarnished by arbitrarily withholding it, its
occupancy from the members of any religious
group. I believe in a President whose views
on religion are his own private affair,

neither imposed upon him by the nation or
imposed by the nation upon him as a condition
to holding that office.

10   I would not look with favor upon a
President working to subvert the First
Amendment's guarantees of religious liberty
(nor would our system of checks and balances
permit him to do so). And neither do I look
with favor upon those who would work to
subvert Article VI of the Constitution by
requiring a religious test--even by
indirection--for if they disagree with that
safeguard, they should be openly working to
repeal it.

11   I want a chief executive whose public
acts are responsible to all and obligated to
none--who can attend any ceremony, service or
dinner his office may appropriately require
him to fulfill--and whose fulfillment of his
Presidential office is not limited or
conditioned by any religious oath, ritual or
obligation.

12   This is the kind of America I believe
in--and this is the kind of America I fought
for in the South Pacific and the kind my
brother died for in Europe. No one suggested
then that we might have a "divided loyalty,"
that we did "not believe in liberty" or that
we belonged to a disloyal group that
threatened "the freedoms for which our
forefathers died."

13   And in fact this is the kind of America
for which our forefathers did die when they
fled here to escape religious test oaths,
that denied office to members of less favored
churches, when they fought for the
Constitution, the Bill of Rights, the
Virginia Statute of Religious Freedom--and
when they fought at the shrine I visited
today--the Alamo. For side by side with
Bowie and Crockett died Fuentes and
McCafferty and Bailey and Bedillio and
Carey--but no one knows whether they were
Catholics or not. For there was no religious
test there.

14   I ask you tonight to follow in that
tradition, to judge me on the basis of
fourteen years in the Congress--on my
declared stands against an ambassador to the

Vatican, against unconstitutional aid to
parochial schools, and against any boycott of
the public schools (which I attended
myself)--and instead of doing this do not
judge me on the basis of these pamphlets and
publications we have all seen that carefully
select quotations out of context from the
statements of Catholic Church leaders,
usually in other countries, frequently in
other centuries, and rarely relevant to any
situation here--and always omitting, of
course, the statement of the American bishops
in 1948 which strongly endorsed church-state
separation, and which more nearly reflects
the views of American Catholics.

15   I do not consider these other quotations
binding upon my public acts--why should you?
But let me say, with respect to other
countries, that I am wholly opposed to the
state being used by any religious group,
Catholic or Protestant, to compel, prohibit
or prosecute the free exercise of any other
religion. And that goes for any persecution
at any time, by anyone, in any country.

16   And I hope that you and I condemn with
equal fervor those nations which deny their
Presidency to Protestants and those which
deny it to Catholics. And rather than cite
the misdeeds of those who differ, I would
also cite the record of the Catholic Church
in such nations as France and Ireland--and
the independence of such statesmen as de
Gaulle and Adenauer.

17   But let me stress again that these are
my views--for, contrary to common newspaper
usage, I am not the Catholic candidate for
President. I am the Democratic party's
candidate for President who happens also to
be a Catholic.

18   I do not speak for my church on public
matters--and the church does not speak for
me.

19   Whatever issue may come before me as
President, if I should be elected--on birth
control, divorce, censorship, gambling, or
any other subject--I will make my decision in
accordance with these views, in accordance
with what my conscience tells me to be in the
national interest, and without regard to

outside religious pressure or dictate. And no power or threat of punishment could cause me to decide otherwise.

20   But if the time should ever come--and I do not concede any conflict to be remotely possible--when my office would require me to either violate my conscience, or violate the national interest, then I would resign the office, and I hope any other conscientious public servant would do likewise.

21   But I do not intend to apologize for these views to my critics of either Catholic or Protestant faith, nor do I intend to disavow either my views or my church in order to win this election. If I should lose on the real issues, I shall return to my seat in the Senate satisfied that I tried my best and was fairly judged.

22   But if this election is decided on the basis that 40,000,000 Americans lost their chance of being President on the day they were baptized, then it is the whole nation that will be the loser in the eyes of Catholics and non-Catholics around the world, in the eyes of history, and in the eyes of our own people.

23   But if, on the other hand, I should win this election, then I shall devote every effort of mind and spirit to fulfilling the oath of the Presidency--practically identical, I might add, with the oath I have taken for fourteen years in the Congress. For, without reservation, I can, and I quote, "solemnly swear that I will faithfully execute the office of President of the United States and will to the best of my ability preserve, protect and defend the Constitution, so help me God."

PRESCRIPTIONS FOR AN OLD PROBLEM

Kimberly Fisher

(This speech was delivered by Kimberly Fisher during the 1989 annual competition of the Interstate Oratorical Association. At the time, Fisher was a student at Arizona State University.)

----

1   Carl Hartman was once an inspiration to his neighbors in the retirement community of Sun City. Even at age 82, he walked for two hours daily, volunteered time at church and served as secretary-treasurer of the Homeowners' Association. In October, 1983, Carl entered the Barrow Neurological Institute for some routine tests. He should have resumed a normal life a few days later. Instead, Carl died. Carl died because the Institute's poorly trained staff mistakenly gave him a deadly dosage of a powerful sedative.

2   Sadly, this story is not unique. An award-winning study conducted last spring by The Arizona Republic, and published in its June 28th edition, revealed that each year 1.9 million older Americans are hospitalized for prescription-related problems, and over 100 of those people die every single day. Some older people, like Carl, are the victims of medical errors. Others unintentionally jeopardize their health by improperly using prescriptions. These related tragedies will kill more Americans in this year alone than the total number of U.S. service people who died in the Vietnam War.

3   The U.S. Census Bureau reports that by the year 2025, one out of every seven Americans will be 60 or older. This problem affects our parents and grandparents, and, if we fail to act, it will one day affect all of us.

4   If we are to end this medication crisis, we must first understand the problem, including its magnitude and the roles played by the primary contributors to it--the medical community and the federal government. Second, we must examine the steps we need to

take to ensure that Carl's tragedy does not afflict our own friends and relatives.

5   Older Americans have greatly expanded their use of prescriptions. Richard Kusserow, the Inspector General of the Department of Health and Human Services, discovered after a February, 1989, study that the elderly consume more than 30 percent of all prescriptions filled in this country, even though they constitute only 17 percent of the U.S. population.

6   Current federal regulations do not even require hospitals or pharmaceutical companies to test for the specific effects prescriptions may have on older patients. As a result, reports Dr. Sidney Wolfe after a 1987 study for the Public Citizen Health Research Group, of the 287 medications most commonly prescribed for the elderly, one-third pose health risks to people over age 55.

7   Even when they receive appropriate prescriptions, the elderly themselves frequently misuse their medications. A 1988 study produced by The National Council On Patient Information and Education, discovered that 50 percent of elderly Americans deliberately disregard the instructions that accompany their prescriptions. Many older people fail to recognize the dangers inherent in such seemingly benign transgressions as sharing prescriptions with friends to save money. Larry Hodge, an administrator at the geriatric Life Care Center in Erwin, Tennessee, reports that nursing homes have frequently admitted patients who were so zonked out from prescription misuse, that "during their meals their heads were in their mashed potatoes."

8   At this point you are probably wondering how a problem of this magnitude escaped the attention of medical experts and even Geraldo Rivera until only the last few weeks. By examining the roles played by the primary contributors to this crisis, we shall see that the answer is sheer ignorance.

9   As we grow older, our metabolisms slow and our ability to tolerate medication decreases. Doctors should learn to adjust

prescriptions to meet the changing needs of their older patients; however, The Arizona Republic's 1988 study found that only two percent of U.S. medical students are required to take courses in geriatrics. When these untrained doctors enter the work force, warns an editorial in the January, 1989, edition of The Journal of the American Geriatric Society, they frequently attribute their patient's prescription-related problems to disease and old age. Consequently, millions of older Americans die needlessly each year because our medical schools and hospitals see little value in teaching doctors to properly prescribe medications.

10   Federal officials are not unaware of this problem. In fact, the issue is frequently debated on the floors of Congress and "studied" by the executive branch. Unfortunately, our government sees a different bottom line: the dollar sign. Drugs are cheaper than alternative treatments, and, in this age of budget deficits, federal officials frequently equate the cheapest solutions with the best. Administrator Larry Hodge notes that current Medicare and Medicaid allotments for nursing home care pay for little more than the drugs needed to keep older patients sedated and out of trouble.

11   Medications will continue to claim the lives of older Americans unless we step in and solve the problem. The logical place to begin is with the initial source: over-prescribing doctors. Last fall, the American Boards of Internal Medicine and Family Practice developed a test to certify doctors in geriatrics. The January 19, 1989, edition of The New England Journal of Medicine reports that hospitals and medical schools have recently prioritized the study of geriatric prescription use.

12   Ideally, the federal government should capitalize on these trends and require all doctors who work with the elderly to receive geriatric training. However, experience demonstrates that, even after extensive public prodding, national agencies seldom do what is ideal. It is, therefore, our responsibility to check into the backgrounds of those doctors treating our older friends

to ensure that the elderly are receiving the best possible care. After all, even long-time family physicians may not be qualified to work with older patients.

13   Even more importantly, we must persuade the elderly themselves to confront this problem head-on. Older people must learn to properly use medications. The National Council on Patient Information and Education advises the elderly to ask their doctors a series of questions before using prescriptions. Briefly summarized, the National Council's recommendations caution older people to never combine prescriptions with additional medication.

14   The February 15, 1989, edition of The New York Times notes that many older people become overmedicated after consulting a different doctor for each problem they develop, and amassing collections of incompatible prescriptions. To combat this level of the crisis, many national drug store chains have established computer networks which can automatically reference a patient's recent prescription history, and alert pharmacists if a new prescription may cause adverse reactions. You can help to reduce the medication crisis by insisting that your older friends use only those pharmacies which provide this service.

15   In addition, we must encourage the elderly to refrain from mixing prescriptions with over-the-counter medications. Patricia Trainor, a project coordinator at the Westchester Clearinghouse, warns that 90 percent of older Americans using prescriptions also take an average of three over-the-counter medications at the same time. The April, 1989, edition of Geriatric Nursing reports that combining prescriptions with such common medicines as aspirin, Pepto-Bismol, or even vitamins, can cause deadly reactions. Consequently, we must persuade the elderly to maintain open channels of communication with their doctors while they are taking any medications.

16   I find it tragically ironic that, in this age of advanced medical technology, the elderly are dying from the very medications that were designed to enhance their lives.

This epidemic has already claimed the lives of Carl Hartman and millions like him.

17   Now that we have examined the scope and causes of the prescription crisis, we must be willing to take the steps necessary to end it. If we fail to act, People like Carl--people like our own parents and grandparents--will be the next victims.

APPENDIX I

SOURCES OF RESOURCES

Sources of Videos and Filmstrips

Here are the addresses of the distributors of the videos and filmstrips listed in the "Resources" sections of Part III of this manual.

1.   The Center for New American Media
     524 Broadway, 2nd Floor
     New York, N. Y. 10012-4408

     This company offers "American Tongues," the video about regional and social dialects in the United States. A descriptive brochure about this program is available.

2.   Coronet/MTI Film & Video
     108 Wilmot Rd.
     Deerfield, Ill. 60015

     Coronet/MTI distributes a variety of videos that concern public speaking, including "Aids to Speaking," "Communication by Voice and Action," and "Planning Your Speech." Write for the Communication brochure.

3.   The Educational Video Group
     374 Shadow Rd.
     Greenwood, Ind. 46142

     This company currently offers a 5-volume set of tapes in its "Great Speeches Series." It also has a textbook on speech criticism. Future plans include videos on "Modern Presidential Campaigns," "The Media Presidents," "Successful Communication," and "Persuasion." A catalog is available.

4.   Films for the Humanities
     P.O. Box 2053
     Princeton, N. J. 08542

     Films for the Humanities offers a set of 28 sound filmstrips in its "Speech and Communication" series. A student workbook, Speaking for Yourself, goes with the series. A brochure summarizing the content of each filmstrip is available.

5.   Kantola-Skeie Productions
      1612 Lyon St.
      San Francisco, Calif. 94115

This company distributes "Be Prepared to Speak," a
video guide to public speaking prepared by Toastmasters
International.

The Speech Communication Association as a
Source of Instructional Aids

The Speech Communication Association (SCA), the
national organization for speech communication
professionals, offers a variety of resource material for the
teacher of public speaking. Here is the address, plus a
brief list of what is available.

            Speech Communication Association
                 5105 Backlick Rd., #E
                 Annandale, Va. 22003

Journals. SCA publishes a variety of communication
journals, including Communication Education, and the Speech
Communication Teacher. Write for current subscription
rates.

Booklet on Speech Evaluation. SCA offers a 42-page
booklet on Evaluating Classroom Speaking, by Douglas G. Bock
and E. Hope Bock. The booklet covers theory and research
concerning speech evaluation, and offers practical
suggestions for the public speaking teacher. A variety of
critique forms are included. Write for current cost.

Annotated Bibliographies. SCA has prepared a variety
of annotated bibliographies concerning speech communication.
Among those bibliographies that should appeal to teachers of
public speaking: "Bibliography of Video Tape Resources in
Speech Communication," by Sue D. Pendell; "Ethical
Responsibility in Communication," by Richard L. Johannesen;
"Persuasion," by Steven T. McDermott; "Persuasion:
Attitude/Behavior Change," by William L. Benoit; "The Theory
of Rhetorical Criticism," by William L. Benoit and Michael
D. Moeder; and "Voice and Articulation," by Willie B.
Morgan. Write for a free copy of each.

Publications List. SCA has available a current list of
publications covering a variety of topics, such as "Teaching
Resources," "Monographs, Proceedings, Reports," "Video
Cassettes," and "Selected Audio Cassettes." The list is
updated each year. Write for a free copy.

APPENDIX II

ANSWERS TO EXAMINATION QUESTIONS

(Note: The answers to all multiple-choice and short answer questions are given below, chapter by chapter. The discussion and essay questions are not answered here; however, each one is referenced to the pages in the text where the answer can be found.)

Chapter 1
The Study of Public Speaking in a Democracy

Multiple-Choice

1. b, Corax

2. d, Aristotle

3. c, ethos

4. c, emotional

5. a, Rhetorica ad Herennium

6. e, ethical proof

7. b, inventio

8. a, elocutio

9. c, Rhetorica ad Herennium

10. a, Hugh Blair

11. c, George Campbell

12. e, Richard Whately

13. d, John Quincy Adams

14. a, The beginning of the twentieth century

15. c, Charles H. Woolbert

Short Answer

16. Aristotle defines rhetoric as "the faculty of discovering in the particular case what are the available means of persuasion." Paraphrase acceptable. (p. 6)

17. Three elements of ethos: (a) good will (friendliness and sincerity); (b) intelligence (knowledge of the subject, expertise); (c) good moral character. (p. 6)

18. Inventio defined: the discovery of speech content; the art of finding proofs. (p. 7)

19. Dispositio defined: the art of speech organization. (p. 7)

20. Elocutio defined: style; the art of using language effectively in speaking. (p. 7)

21. Pronuntiatio defined: delivery; the use of voice and body in speaking. (p. 7)

22. Author of the Institutes of Oratory: Quintilian. (p. 8)

23. Author of De Oratore: Cicero. (p. 8)

24. "Lost canon of rhetoric": memoria (memory). (p. 7)

25. Three English rhetoricians: Hugh Blair, George Campbell, and Richard Whately. (p. 9)

Discussion and Essay

26. Corax in Syracuse, p. 5.

27. Aristotle's three forms of proof, p. 6.

28. Discuss statement on free society, pp. 12-13, and from Chapter 1 in general.

Chapter 2
Your First Speeches

Multiple-Choice

1.   b, audience attitudes

2.   b, the general purpose

3.   d, specific purpose

4.   b, for all points

5.   b, central idea

6.   e, specific example

7.   d, general purpose

8.   a, chronological

9.   c, directly into the eyes of the listeners

10.   e, thoroughly master speech content

Short Answer

11.   Audience analysis includes: knowledge and attitudes.
      (p. 19)

12.   Three of four types of supporting material: examples,
      comparison and contrast, and authority (testimony).
      (p. 22)

13.   Total number of main points: two to five. (p. 23)

14.   Complete the statement: [Fear of public speaking
      emerges from a personal assessment that] "your
      speaking ability falls short of audience expectations."
      Paraphrase accepted. (p. 29)

15.   Complete the statement: [Fear of public speaking is
      intensified when the speaker believes that] "important
      inadequacies will be revealed." (p. 29)

Discussion and Essay

16.   Explain broad and narrowed subject, p. 20.

17.   Explain specific purpose and central idea, p. 21.

18.   Do a component parts example, p. 24.

19. Do a topical example, p. 24.

20. Discuss "imaginary" vs. "real" problems of speech anxiety, p. 30.

Chapter 3
Democratic Values, Free Speech, and Speaker Ethics

Multiple-Choice

1. d, sedition laws

2. b, blasphemy laws

3. c, Brandenburg v. Ohio

4. a, defamation

5. b, a person is strict and uncompromising

6. d, public places must be open for marches and demonstrations, but their use is subject to reasonable regulation

7. b, academic freedom is not a constitutional right, but it is a good thing for American education

8. b, Quintilian

9. c, Greece

10. c, should be based on a belief sincerely held by the speaker

Short Answer

11. Two additional democratic values: human capacity to reason (critical capacity), and equality. (pp. 38-39)

12. Three additional assumptions of democracy: freedom of speech, decision by majority vote, and respect for minority rights. (p. 39)

13. Two additional areas of ethical responsibility: to speech content, and to society at large. (pp. 48-49)

Discussion and Essay

14. Brandenburg rule explained, p. 41.

15. Discuss slander and libel, p. 42.

16. Discuss criticism of religion, pp. 42-43.

Chapter 4
The Communication Process and Listening

Multiple-Choice

1. e, the channel

2. c, within the members of the audience

3. b, 25%

4. c, 50%

5. b, a political campaign speech

6. e, about 3 to 4 times faster

7. c, chronological

8. e, postponing decision making

9. a, voice and body over soundwaves and lightwaves

10. b, credibility

Short Answer

11. To complete definition of communication: attitudes and feelings. (p. 56)

12. Function of words: stir up meaning already present within the mind of each listener. (p. 58)

13. Remaining six elements in communication model (in correct order): message, channel, receiver, feedback, interference, and situation. (pp. 56-57)

Discussion and Essay

14. Explain feedback, source, and interference, pp. 56-60.

15. Explain one way reading and listening differ, p. 61.

16. Explain "listen past delivery" and "the speech-thought differential," pp. 62-63.

Chapter 5
Analyzing the Audience and Occasion

Multiple-Choice

1. d, audience interests

2. b, attitudes

3. c, Aristotle

4. c, educated

5. d, attitude on the subject

6. a, beliefs and values

7. a, open-ended

8. b, values

9. c, establish rapport and good will

10. a, attitude on the topic

Short Answer

11. Remaining three parts of occasion analysis: audience
    size, meeting facilities, and whether broadcasting or
    not. (pp. 81-82)

12. Remaining two ways of gathering information: ask
    questions, and administer questionnaires. (pp. 83-84)

13. One thing audience analysis should not do: (either one
    of the following is acceptable) should not cause
    speaker to compromise convinctions; or, should not be
    thought of as a "secret weapon" for brainwashing the
    audience. (pp. 72-73)

Discussion and Essay

14. Define and explain "attitude," p. 75.

15. How to analyze the occasion, pp. 81-82.

16. Use of demographic information, pp. 78-80.

17. Define and discuss "common ground," pp. 86-87.

18. How to address a hostile audience, pp. 86-88.

Chapter 6
Determining the Subject and Purpose

Multiple-Choice

1. d, broad subject

2. b, specific purpose

3. c, change-of-behavior speech

4. a, limited to that which amuses

5. c, specific purpose

6. c, specific purpose

7. b, may include both entertaining and informative content

8. c, central idea

9. e, central idea of a persuasive speech

10. a, central idea of an informative speech

Short Answer

11. Subject appropriate to three things: speaker, audience, and occasion. (p. 98)

12. Three general purposes: to entertain, inform, and persuade. (pp. 102-103)

13. Subjects can be found in: problems (or in problems and their solutions). (pp. 96-98)

Discussion and Essay

14. Difference between specific purpose and central idea, pp. 103-106.

15. Explain differences in entertaining, informing, and persuading, pp. 102-103.

Chapter 7
Supporting Materials for Public Speeches

Multiple-Choice

1. b, accurate, relevant, and clear

2. c, hypothetical example

3. a, figurative analogy

4. d, the mean

5. a, the median

6. d, authoritative statement

7. c, tell audience the qualifications of person
    testifying

8. a, avoid hypothetical examples

9. a, analogy

10. a, a simple average

Short Answer

11. Three functions of supporting materials: interest,
    clarity, and persuasiveness. (p. 112)

12. "Average" of least use: the mode. (p. 118)

13. Three tests of examples: have enough examples, use
    real examples (not hypothetical), use typical examples.
    (p. 115)

14. Two tests of comparison and contrast: base on facts,
    and comparisons should be alike in essential details.
    (p. 117)

15. Three tests of statistics: accuracy, from reliable
    source, and recent. (pp. 118-119)

16. Three tests of authority: should be qualified, be fair
    and objective, and should be supported by other
    authorities and other forms of evidence. (pp. 121-122)

Discussion and Essay

17. Explain examples, comparison and contrast, statistics,
    and authority, pp. 114-121.

18. Discuss: "present statistics in a form that facilitates understanding," p. 120.

19. Advice on using statistics well, pp. 117-120.

20. Explain meaning of "qualify your source," p. 121.

Chapter 8
Research: Finding Speech Materials

Multiple-Choice

1. b, Library of Congress Subject Headings

2. d, do a key word search

3. c, Readers' Guide to Periodical Literature

4. a, The National Newspaper Index

5. c, the newspaper indexes

6. a, Dictionary of American Biography

7. d, Monthly Catalog of U.S. Government Publications

8. b, The Gallup Report

9. d, Statistical Abstract of the United States

10. c, Encyclopedia of Associations

Short Answer

11. To get materials from other libraries, use: interlibrary loan. (p. 132)

12. What is in The Essay and General Literature Index? Collected (anthologized) essays, by author and title. (p. 134)

13. Microfilm index for magazines: The Magazine Index. (p. 134)

14. American newspaper indexed since 1851: The New York Times. (p. 136)

15. Weekly summary of current events: Facts on File (Facts on File Yearbook is cumulated annually). (p. 138)

Discussion and Essay

16. Computer search, pp. 139-140.

17. Interviewing, pp. 140-143.

18. Explain systematic browsing, p. 145.

19. Use of encyclopedias, p. 145.

Chapter 9
Introducing Outlining: Three Practical Concepts

Multiple-Choice

1.   e, dispositio

2.   b, a statement and support for that statement

3.   a, only one

4.   c, the body of the speech

5.   a, they are subordinate

6.   b, speech units

7.   b, a superior point

8.   d, the "for" test

9.   d, the "also" test

10. c, when speaking time is short in a persuasive speaking situation

Short Answer

11. Complete the sentence: [One of the standard rules of outlining is that each point should be stated as] a complete sentence (or as one short, complete sentence). (p. 153)

12. Main points function as: subpoints (or subordinate points). (pp. 156-157)

13. Two parts of speech unit: a (general) statement, and support for that (general) statement. (p. 154)

14. Two equal subpoints: coordinate. (p. 159)

Discussion and Essay

15. Explain the speech unit, pp. 154-158.

16. Explain "a speech has one and only one main point, and that is the central idea," pp. 156-157.

17. Explain "for" and "also" tests, pp. 160-163.

18. When one supporting point is logical, pp. 164-166.

Chapter 10
Organizing and Outlining the Body of the Speech

Multiple-Choice

1. b, two to five

2. c, topical

3. a, chronological

4. c, component parts

5. c, topics inherent in the subject

6. d, the motivated sequence

7. a, state key reasons

8. a, component parts

9. d, problem-solution

10. c, evidence

Short Answer

11. Goal of speech to inform: to achieve understanding. (p. 176)

12. Goal of speech to persuade: to modify attitudes and behavior (in ways intended by the speaker). (p. 180)

13. Function of subpoints in informative outline: to present the parts of the whole (or break the subject or topic into digestible pieces of discourse). (p. 176)

14. Function of subpoints in persuasive outline: to prove the point under which they fall (or state subreasons and give evidence). (pp. 187-188)

Discussion and Essay

15. Difference in function of main points in informing and persuading, pp. 176 and 180.

16. Five steps of motivated sequence, pp. 184-185.

17. Explain "inherent" and "created" topics, pp. 178-179.

18. Climax and anti-climax orders, pp. 186-187.

Chapter 11
Introductions, Conclusions, and Transitions

Multiple-Choice

1. b, about 10% of the speech

2. a, between 5% and 10% of the speech

3. c, a question to which the answer is obvious

4. e, speaker credibility with the audience

5. c, place it where it will be most effective

6. e, ending the speech in a creative way

7. e, transitions

8. b, state the key argument and prove it

9. c, verbal signposts

10. b, ethos

Short Answer

11. Three goals of the introduction: catch attention and interest, establish speaker credibility, and win an intelligent hearing. (p. 199)

12. Two goals of the conclusion: focus on and reinforce key points, and wrap up speech creatively. (p. 208)

13. Two functions of transitions: for smooth movement from point to point, and to call attention to important points. (p. 212)

<u>Discussion and Essay</u>

14. Discuss the problems of introductions to persuasive speeches, p. 104.

15. Discuss the problems of conclusions to persuasive speeches, p. 211.

16. Explain "end the speech with a creative finishing touch," pp. 209-211.

Chapter 12
Language in Public Speaking

<u>Multiple-Choice</u>

1. d, the referent

2. a, stylistic and semantic

3. b, the mind of the listener

4. c, the territory

5. c, the speaker, audience, and occasion

6. e, familiar

7. b, doublespeak

8. a, simile

9. e, antithesis

10. d, alliteration

<u>Short Answer</u>

11. What words do: (as symbols) words stir up meaning already present in the mind of the listener. (p. 221)

12. Three elements of style: appropriateness, clarity, and vividness. (p. 222)

13. Complete the definition: [Communication can be defined as the process by which humans attempt to] <u>share thoughts, attitudes, and feelings with one another</u>. (p. 222)

Discussion and Essay

14. Discuss: "Just as the map is not the territory, the word is not the thing," p. 222.

15. Discuss: "No two people use language in exactly the same way," p. 221.

16. Discuss sexist language, p. 223.

17. Explain "vividness" in language, pp. 226-230.

Chapter 13
Delivering the Speech

Multiple-Choice

1. b, impromptu

2. c, quality

3. a, extemporaneous

4. e, stand back 12 to 15 inches from the mike

5. c, 125 to 175

6. e, articulation

7. b, current usage by the leaders of society

8. d, the eyes

9. a, practice delivery several times while standing

10. a, enunciation

Short Answer

11. Define impromptu speaking: spur-of-the-moment delivery, without any prior preparation. (pp. 238-239)

12. Define extemporaneous speaking: carefully prepared in advance, but not memorized or read (usually delivered from notes). (pp. 236-237)

13. Four of the six physical elements of delivery: visual directness, posture, movement, and gesture. (pp. 245-248).

14. Indistinct, distorted speech sounds are problems of: articulation. (p. 244)

Discussion and Essay

15. Explain the four types of speech presentation, pp. 236-239.

16. Explain the four elements of the voice, pp. 141-243.

17. Difference between articulation and pronunciation, pp. 243-245.

18. Use of a key word note card, pp. 236-237, and 249.

19. Essay on "Effective Bodily Communication in Public Speaking," pp. 245-249.

Chapter 14
Speaking to Inform

Multiple-Choice

1. d, achieve understanding

2. b, speech about processes and procedures

3. c, use both positive and negative incentives

4. d, use positive incentives

5. b, negative incentive

6. e, statistics

7. a, motivation

8. b, satisfy curiosity

9. c, retention of information

10. b, speech about objects and areas

Short Answer

11. Explain the unfamiliar in terms of: the familiar. (p. 266)

12. Three objectives of informing: motivation, clarity, and retention. (pp. 262-263)

13. Basic goal of informing: to achieve understanding (or, to explain a subject to the audience so that the audience achieves understanding). (p. 256)

Discussion and Essay

14. Compare goals of informing and persuading, p. 256.

15. Place of informing in a democracy, pp. 257-258.

16. Explain the three objectives of informing, pp. 262-267.

Chapter 15
The Means of Persuasion

Multiple-Choice

1.   c, induction

2.   e, good character

3.   b, appeal to emotions

4.   b, deductive

5.   c, ethos

6.   a, a syllogism

7.   e, parallel case

8.   c, prior ethos

9.   d, physiological

10. b, human values

Short Answer

11. Complete the definition: [persuasive speaking is
     spoken discourse that] is planned so as to modify
     beliefs, values, attitudes, and behavior in directions
     intended by the speaker. (p. 274)

12. Three standards of evidence: be accurate, clear, and
     relevant. (p. 276)

13. Two tests of induction: need an adequate number of
     instances, and the instances should be typical. (pp.
     278-279)

14. Two tests of deduction: premises must be proved (that
     is, must be true), and the conclusion must follow
     logically from the premises. (p. 281)

15. Two tests of parallel case: information on the cases must be accurate, and the things being compared must be alike in essential details. (pp. 284-285)

16. Any two of the three tests of causal reasoning: (take two) must be a genuine connection between cause and effect; determine if there is a single cause, or multiple causes (and which is most significant); and cause must be strong enough to produce the claimed effect. (p. 283)

17. Give two examples of positive and two of negative emotions (any two of each):
    positive--joy, relief, elation, happiness, patriotism, and the like.
    negative--fear, anger, sympathy, pity, sorrow, shame, and the like. (p. 289)

Discussion and Essay

18. Explain logical proof, pp. 275-285.

19. Explain ethical proof (credibility), pp. 285-288.

20. Explain pathos (psychological appeals), pp. 288-293.

21. Explain "qualifying your source," p. 276.

22. Explain Maslow's heirarchy of needs, pp. 289-291.

23. Explain Rokeach's value system, pp. 292-293.

Chapter 16
Speaking to Persuade

Multiple-Choice

1. c, to actuate

2. b, to convince

3. d, reinforce

4. c, to convince

5. e, to reinforce

6. b, mental agreement

7. c, pathos

8. d, observable

9.   c, to reinforce

10. c, cognitive consistency

Short Answer

11. Two of three methods of getting others to do what you want: bribery and persuasion. (p. 300)

12. Attitude defined: The predisposition of a person to evaluate an issue (action, object, symbol, person, or situation) in a favorable or unfavorable way. (p. 300)

13. Attitude calling for speech to convince: unfavorable (opposed; disagree). (p. 301)

14. Attitude calling for speech to actuate: favorable (support; agree). (p. 304)

15. Attitude suitable for speech to reinforce: favorable (support, in agreement). (p. 307)

Discussion and Essay

16. Discuss speech to convince, pp. 301-303.

17. Discuss speech to actuate, pp. 303-307.

18. Discuss speech to reinforce, pp. 307-309.

19. Explain argument/counter-argument, pp. 311-312.

20. Explain cognitive consistency, 312-314.

21. Explain reward/penalty, pp. 314-315.

Chapter 17
Special Forms and Occasions

Multiple-Choice

1.   c, to inspire

2.   d, eulogy

3.   b, to actuate

4.   a, past events or accomplishments

5.   d, good will

6.   d, nomination

7.   d, actuate

8.   b, inspirational

9.   e, entertaining

10. c, eulogy

Short Answer

11. Types of speech called for:

a.   In honor of Martin Luther King, <u>a eulogy</u> (pp. 323-324)
b.   By senior at graduation, <u>celebration</u> (p. 324)

c.   Outstanding debater, <u>presentation</u> (p. 330)

12. Three standards of speeches of courtesy: should not be tightly organized, should be positive and pleasant, and should be short. (p. 327)

Discussion and Essay

13. Explain the eulogy, pp. 323-324.

14. Explain the speech of good will, pp. 325-327.

15. Explain preparation of speech of introduction, pp. 327-329.

16. Explain the speech to entertain, pp. 330-332.

Appendix I
Speech Criticism: Analyzing and
Evaluating Public Speeches

Short Answer

1.   Define speech criticism: informed, fair-minded analysis and evaluation of a speech. (p. 336)

2.   Speech evaluation should assess (three things): effectiveness, artistic quality (aesthetics), and social worth (ethics, social consequences). (pp. 337-339)

3. Bitzer's definition of "exigence": an imperfection marked by urgency (or, an urgent need, a defect calling for correction, an urgent problem that calls for a solution). (p. 345)

4. One reason for a speech is to address a human problem or need; what is a second reason? To comply with tradition. (pp. 345-346)

Discussion and Essay

5. Explain "speech analysis," p. 336.

6. Discuss the evaluation of "effectiveness," pp. 337-338.

7. Discuss the evaluation of "artistic quality," p. 338.

8. Discuss the evaluation of "social worth," pp. 338-339.

NOTES

NOTES